MARIO PAGANO

HERCULANEUM

A REASONED ARCHAEOLOGICAL ITINERARY

Translated by Angelo Pesce

Charles (later Charles III) of
Bourbon, a portrait from the book
Le antichità di Ercolano

© 2000 Copyright T&M srl
ISBN 88-87150-04-4

Supervision Annibale Illario
Printed in Italy by SBR srl - Portici (Na)
Photographies L. Butler, E. Lupoli, G. Massimo, archives V. Catalano, under
licence of Ministero per i Beni Culturali e Ambientali - Soprintendenza
Archeologica di Pompei.
Drawings and plans: Ubaldo Pastore

Publisher T&M srl - Registered Office: Via Circumvallazione, 137/z
Offices: Via Duca Lecco De Guevara, 17
80059 Torre del Greco (Na) - Italy

Cover: *a view of the scene of Herculaneum theatre where Bourbon excavations started from.*
Back cover: *a marble relief with satyrs and a nymphe drawing off a spring - Herculaneum west end*
new excavations.

Foreword

We are indebted to Mario Pagano for this "Reasoned Archaeological Itinerary": specialists and visitors will find in it a thought-out and reasonable inventory of what is preserved in Herculaneum, as well as its meaning in archaeology, in ancient history and in the history of art and culture.

The result of the Author's endeavours is a valuable guidebook which helps to apply programmed activity – something which has been already started on the site. This novel approach, with a specific emphasis on the visitors' requirements, will provide Herculaneum with facilities befitting its importance and a more comfortable connection with the modern city.

This guidebook will equally benefit the concerned archaeologists, who are provided with priority inventories, mainly dealing with maintenance and restoration of what has been found up to now; although the somewhat ill-considered speed in the new excavations of Villa of the Papyri necessarily requires a great share of the available funds in order to normalise the situation in the western suburban sector.

Lastly, this book reminds us that among the aims of scientific research there is also that of making the non-specialised public aware of the results of new research programs, so that they may gradually enter the domain of general culture.

There is still much to do in order to achieve satisfactory knowledge of ancient Herculaneum. In this attempt we hope to continue to meet public consent and participation.

Pietro Giovanni Guzzo
Archaeological Superintendent of Pompeii

"The three Herculaneum ladies", found by the prince d'Elboeuf in 1711 on the Theatre scene in Herculaneum (*Photographs courtesy of Dresden Museum*)

INTRODUCTION

The name of Herculaneum is strictly bound not only to the history of archaeology but also to the history of European culture. It was here that, in 1738, the fruitful Vesuvian excavations began, and the unearthed treasures marked the artistic taste of an era. Currently surviving in the shadow of nearby Pompeii, but still visited by more than 230,000 tourists a year (their numbers showing a steady increase), Herculaneum is appreciated for its secluded tranquillity and for its better-preserved house walls, and even the delicate wooden structures of the buildings. Thanks to the plans already started for the opening of a new and more comfortable entrance from the east, directly connected with the Naples-Salerno motorway, Herculaneum is now moving towards the inclusion of the Theatre in the visitors' circuit, the opening of the antiquarium, the replacing on-site of casts of the countless objects found and of the sculptures, mosaics and inscriptions taken away in the 18th century, and finally the full excavation of Villa of the Papyri, with the aim of attracting renewed worldwide attention.

After the guidebook of the great archaeologist Amedeo Maiuri, last published in 1958, a more detailed, up to date and handy guide was sorely needed, which could inform the visitor about the considerable progress of knowledge gained during recent years and the stunning latest discoveries.

After over ten years of work in this unique archaeological site, during which time I have conducted new studies and productive research, I would like to introduce this booklet, hopefully aimed, with its clear and fluent language, to a larger public. My fondest hope is that it will not only be found useful as a guide to visit Herculaneum, but also as a starting point for possible deeper investigations.

I leave it to the reader to judge whether or not I have been up to my task.

Mario Pagano
Director of Herculaneum Excavations

Both myself and the translator, my friend of long standing Angelo Pesce, wish to express deep gratitude to Catharin Welligan Panariello for her kind final proofing of the English text

PRACTICAL INFORMATION

The archaeological excavations of Herculaneum can be easily reached by car from Naples, the usual point of arrival for tourists from abroad, exiting the Napoli-Salerno motorway at Ercolano.

The "Circumvesuviana" train lines from Naples, departing from "Corso Garibaldi" or "Piazza Garibaldi" at the Central Railway Station, are fast and comfortable, and all trains stop at Ercolano, served by both the Napoli-Sorrento and the Napoli-Poggiomarino lines. As to the latter, the visitor must be sure to take the train via Pompeii and <u>not</u> via Ottaviano, which also goes to Poggiomarino, but from the <u>other</u> side of Vesuvius. The State Railway, also from "Piazza Garibaldi", is less comfortable and slower; the closest station is that by the name of "Portici-Granatello". In the same category of service is the trolley bus line, departing from the same place but having a stop by the entrance to the excavations.

Tourists can advantageously visit the archaeological site and make the traditional ascent to the crater of Vesuvius, thanks to a service provided by buses leaving from the "Circumvesuviana" station square in Ercolano.

Father Antonio Piaggio from Genoa, inventor of the first device for unrolling papyri.

6

HISTORY OF THE CITY

The ancient historian Dionysius of Halicarnassus mentions a mythical settlement founded by Hercules while he was skirting the Campanian coast guiding the herds seized in Spain from the giant Geryon. The Augustan age geographer Strabo asserts that the city, named after its founder, had a history similar to that of Pompeii. In the city the Opici-Oscans, the Etruscans, the legendary Pelagians and finally the Samnites succeeded each other before the Romans took over the control of the region at the end of the 4th century B.C. Nevertheless, recent discoveries from deep excavations carried out in various points of the urban area have shown that the city was planned only during the first part of the 4th century B.C. Even if an older core existed, it must have been much smaller than the city subdivided into rectangular plots, and perhaps located in its still unexcavated uphill section. With Pompeii and Stabiae, the city was part of the Nucerine confederation. It preserved Oscan culture and language for a long time, as seen from an inscription on a marble altar dedicated to Venus Eryx at the beginning of the 1st century B.C., dug out in the 18th century excavations, now in the epigraphic collection of the National Archaeological Museum in Naples.

During the social war Herculaneum was occupied by the army of the Italic rebels led by Papius Mutilus. Reconquered by a lieutenant of Silla in 89 B.C. it preserved, unlike Pompeii, its municipal legal status, ruled by two magistrates in charge for one year, called *duoviri*. The presence of *aediles*, magistrates who controlled, among other things, the market places, and maintenance and cleaning of streets and public buildings, can be also be attested. A wall inscription confirms the presence, among public servants, of a *quaestor* who was responsible of the city's financial administration. From the 1st century B.C. onwards the Herculaneum coast started to be crowded with large seaside villas owned by Roman aristocrats attracted by the mild climate (Strabo relates that the city was particularly well-exposed to the mitigating influence of the southwesterly *libeccio* wind) and by the nearness of both the Greek city of Naples, a sophisticated cultural centre, and of Pozzuoli, a great business entrepot where merchandise of every kind flowed in from all over the Roman empire. Besides the huge Villa of the Papyri, those of Calastro and Sora in Torre del Greco are well known, as well as those of the Regal Stables, of the Epitaph and of the place known as "the Jesuits' convent" (now hosting the Secondary School "Macedonio Melloni") in Portici. The same Strabo, perhaps with a bit of hyperbole, describes the coast of the Bay of Naples as so dense with buildings as to acquire the aspect of one single city.

Herculaneum's small but fertile territory was famous for specialised cultivation: above all for its vines, but also for a special variety of figs. General renewal of its buildings dates back to the Augustan age, when

Herculaneum
Present general plan of the excavated area with numbers related to blocks and buildings referred to in this guidebook

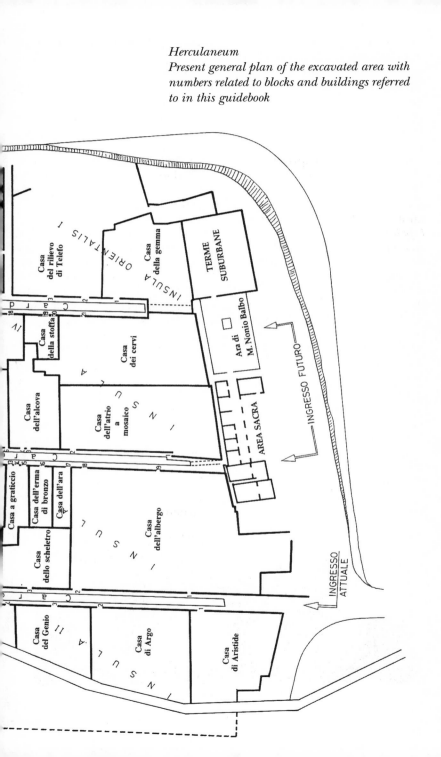

the theatre, the basilica, the aqueduct with its network of public fountains, the market place, the seaside temples, the two thermal establishments and the giant gymnasium complex were built or renovated and the city walls restored. At that time in Herculaneum *M. Nonius Balbus* was the Nucerine senator, praetor (magistrate) and proconsul of Crete and Cyrene; he is remembered in many inscriptions for his benevolent activities.

Leaving aside the debated problem of who the owner of the magnificent Villa of the Papyri was (perhaps it belonged to Julius Caesar's father in law, *L. Calpurnius Piso Cesoninus*), there was somebody else who was very important and had great interest in the city's well-being. His name was *Appius Claudius Pulcher*, consul in 38 B.C. and Cicero's friend. Another great character in the Augustan period was *M'. Aemilius Lepidus*. He owned a villa in the area, because seals with his name, engraved on tiles, have only been found in Herculaneaum. *L. Mammius Pollio*, consul in 49 A.D. who was related to Agrippina, was probably from the city. Another villa in Herculaneum was owned by the large senatorial family of the *Ulpii*. The rich matron Rectina, a friend of Pliny the Elder, who tried to rescue her at the time of the eruption, also inhabited these shores. In the Herculaneum territory there was also a magnificent villa belonging to the imperial family, destroyed by Caligula because his mother Iulia Agrippina had been banished to it.

During the Augustan age the city may have suffered an earthquake, and then again it was hit by a destructive one in 62 A.D., which preceded the great vesuvian eruption of 79 A.D. The historian Seneca clearly states, in connection with the 62 A.D. earthquake, that while Pompeii was totally destroyed, "Herculaneum also partly collapsed and what remains is in danger of falling". Inscriptions proclaim that after this disastrous event, Vespasian financed the restoration of the porticoed square, wrongly called basilica, and the *Mater Magna* (Cybele) temple next to the gymnasium, as yet unexcavated. Other restoration work is visible in the theatre, in the gymnasium, in the suburban thermal baths, in the coastal temples and in many other city structures.

The entrance to the new excavations in Herculaneum

10

THE ERUPTION

On the morning of August 24, 79 A.D., after a long period of quiescence the top of the imposing Vesuvius volcano exploded. The eruption was vividly described, in two letters to the historian Tacitus, by a direct witness of the event: Pliny the Younger, who lived at the time in Miseno with his uncle Pliny the Elder. The latter was a famous naturalist, commander of the imperial Navy, who died on the Stabian seashore after having attempted a rescue mission while the eruption was at its worst.

Since the stratospheric winds were at that time blowing southeastwards, on Herculaneum, unlike Pompeii, only a very thin layer of fallout pumice is found. The initial "glowing avalanche" (or pyroclastic flow) instead, with a temperature of over 400 degrees Celsius, reached Herculaneum at a speed of about 70 to 80 km an hour (about 20 to 22m per second) on the evening of the same day, causing the death of a number of unfortunate fugitives who had crowded into some of the seashore storerooms. During that night "a night blacker than the blackest" (in Pliny's words) and the early morning of August 25 various pyroclastic flows alternating with pyroclastic surges, for a total of at least twelve successive events of this type, covered the city with a layer of ash — mixed with a variety of other materials — between 9 and 21 metres thick. In many parts the ashes underwent a litification process, and were turned into hard tuff. This in most instances makes the Herculanuem worksite more similar to a quarry than to an archaeological excavation. In many cases, though, such circumstances and the thickness of the volcanic layer have produced a better preservation of the upper levels of the buildings, unlike those in Pompeii which were not subjected to complete burial. There is also better preservation of wood and other organic material, which makes visiting Herculaneum very instructive and fascinating, in spite of the fact that the excavated area is rather smaller in comparison.

The eruptive phenomena came to an almost complete standstill on the same day of August 25, but human activities, according to archaeological findings, were resumed in this territory only in the 2nd century A.D.; the place had by then been incorporated into the nearby city of Naples.

Reconstruction of the Theatre scene by F. Mazois

HISTORY OF THE EXCAVATIONS

The discovery of Herculaneum dates back to 1710, although some relics were unearthed in the 16th century (statues placed on the Collimozzi fountain, a bronze plaque with a senate decree, an inscription). A certain farmer, Ambrogio Nocerino nicknamed Enzechetta, while digging a well, found by chance the stage of the Theatre with its very ornate marble façade. A marble-cutter who worked for the prince d'Elbouef, commander of the Austrian imperial armed forces in Naples, was at that time employed in the construction of a beautiful villa nearby, close to the Granatello beach in Portici. He bought the unearthed marble and informed the prince of the discovery, who decided to support the excavation financially for about nine months. The tunnels made then are sketched in a plan of the Theatre drawn by a captain of the Corps of Engineers, Rocco Gioacchino d'Alcubierre. The stage was mostly stripped of its revetment, and many statues, some still standing in their niches when found, were unearthed and taken away. Three of them were sent to Vienna as a gift to Eugene of Savoy and now, after some vicissitudes, are proudly kept in the Dresden Museum. Fragments of other statues placed in Elboeuf's villa at the Granatello, were later moved to the Museum in Portici when the same villa was bought by the Bourbons.

The excavations by d'Elboeuf were discontinued, but after about thirty years d'Alcubierre, who was in the process of mapping the area, having become aware of the shaft, the diggings and the discoveries, asked for, and obtained permission in 1738 to dig more tunnels, while Charles of Bourbon was building the nearby Royal Palace in Portici. Thanks to an inscription, Marcello Venuti identified the building as the Herculaneum Theatre. In 1739 the excavation was extended to the "Spinetta" well, in the so-called Basilica area. The astonishing vesuvian discoveries made Herculaneum very famous in every part of Europe and greatly encouraged the formation and development of the cultural and artistic neoclassic movement. The chance discovery, in 1750, of Villa of the Papyri (also in the course of digging a well) with its sculptures and its library, renewed the interest for excavations by the means of tunnels. But when Charles Weber, the careful, accurate, Swiss military engineer who was the real force behind the Herculaneum underground exploration in those years, died in 1764, he was succeeded by the young Francesco La Vega, and the excavations were limited to a few trials in the Theatre area in order to prepare the publication of scientific reports. In 1780 the excavation was definitively interrupted; in its place attention was given to Pompeii and Stabiae, where results looked more promising and easier to obtain.

Aerial view of Herculaneum (*Photo courtesy of the National Geographic Society*)

A plan to continue the excavations in the early part of the 19th century was not followed through.

It was only during the short reign of Francis I of Bourbon, who had a particular interest in Vesuvian archaeology, that works were resumed in 1828. This time the excavations were carried out in the open air, at the extremity of the third *cardo* towards the sea, and continued with limited resources until 1837, when they were interrupted because of disappointing results. They were started again for a short period between 1850 and 1855. After the unification of Italy (1861), thanks to Giuseppe Fiorelli and the personal financial contribution of King Victor Emmanuel II, between 1869 and 1877 the Herculaneum excavations were resumed once more, only to be definitively interrupted later on.

Herculaneum was taken into consideration again in 1907, when a famous English archaeologist, Charles Waldstein, suggested a vast international endeavour similar to that which brought the Athenian *agora* to light. The Italian government rejected this suggestion, forming instead a committee in charge of the resumption of the excavations, which completed its work in 1909. But again it was only after many years — also due to the outbreak of World War I — that it was possible to resume the excavation efficiently and honorably in 1927, on the initiative of the Fascist regime, under the direction of Amedeo Maiuri and with extraordinary financial support. By 1942 almost all of the open air area, which can be seen at present, was unearthed. After World War II other excavations were made in the Palaestra, in the Suburban Thermae and along the *decumanus maximus*. Particularly, in 1961-62, the Tuscan Colonnade House, the atrium area of the Black Hall House, many shops, the College of the Augustales and the "Basilica" southern end were brought out. Starting in 1981 the excavation of the ancient seashore took place, downhill from the Suburban Thermae and the Temple of Venus. The exploration was progressively developed during the intervening years with an enormous trench going beyond Via Mare, which reaches the southwest end of the city and the area of the atrium of Villa of the Papyri. There is still much to be done, with more adequate tools, also in order to guarantee the preservation of what has been and will be brought to light: particularly the complete unearthing of the Forum area — which is incredibly almost intact — a whole lot of public buildings, and the complete excavation of the Villa of the Papyri, as expected by the international cultural world. Much more is in store, from the progress of studies, the modern tools of research available and the re-examination of the documents unearthed in the 17th century excavations, which are a real mine of information. In this way Herculaneum archaeology will experience a new extraordinary era.

THE ROMAN HOUSE IN HERCULANEUM AND ITS FURNITURE

Perhaps the most important aspect of a visit to Herculaneum is the domestic organisation of the local household, due to the good preservation of walls and wooden furniture. In the city there are important examples of the history of the Roman house evolution through almost three centuries, i.e. from the 2nd century B.C. to the eruption in 79 A.D. If some very small, simple houses had a narrow and long rectangular plan, reflecting the shape of lots and an urban grid from the Oscan age, many examples of the typical, upper-class Roman "atrium house" still remain. This type of house had a vestibule at the entrance, which led on to a big room, at times with pillars (atrium), at times with an opening in the roof (*compluvium*) underlain by a basin for collecting water (*impluvium*), then conveyed to an underground cistern.

In some instances the atrium was completely covered to become a room, in others there was no atrium at all, or it broadened to become a courtyard. All around the atrium there were tiny bedrooms (*cubicula*)

Charred wooden cabinet

which were kept quite small because of the difficulty of heating them but when necessary this was done with stoves and braziers — and other rooms used as living rooms (*alae*). At the back there was a larger room, the *tablinum*, where family archives were kept and where, originally, people used to eat and sit during the summertime, opening up on one side towards the atrium and on the opposite side towards the garden (*hortus*). With the progressive development and enlargement of the houses and the number of their entertainment rooms around the peristyle at the back, the *tablinum* took on the role of reception and socializing hall, a special place where the master of the house would talk with his clients, at times very numerous. Behind the *tablinum*, already from the 3rd - 2nd century B.C., the garden space was monumentalized and surrounded by porticoes leading to large halls (*oeci*), day cubicles, bedrooms, wintertime and summertime triclinia. The servants' quarters were obviously more modest. The kitchen was in many instances also used to contribute to the house-heating and was usually placed next to a small, dark latrine. Only the richer houses had private thermal baths, as the so-called Hotel House did.

Charred wooden table with griffin-shaped legs

Another feature of the houses of a certain standing was a back entrance (*posticum*). Sometimes one or two shops were directly attached to the house, allowing its master to sell his agricultural products, source of the period's wealth. The land available for construction was very scarce, particularly in the city centre, a contingency which soon led to the erection of an upper floor. After the Claudian age there where even buildings on the main road with more than two floors, predecessors of the "high-rise" houses of the 2nd century A.D. in Rome and Ostia. More modest dwellings, divided into many flats, such as the Trellis House, are also present. Since the Augustan age the diminished role of the city walls and the increased opulence encouraged the building of more and more sumptuous houses on the coast facing the delightful Bay of Naples, clearly influenced by the architecture of the huge maritime villas which were already a dominant feature elsewhere on the seafront.

Small bronze statue of an Egyptian god (Bes), an element of furniture

In these villas many architectural novelties of the time can be seen, that is, the presence of big rooms (*oeci*), called Egyptian or Cizicen (from Cizico, a city in Asia Minor), mentioned by Vitruvius. The first type is a big room having a basilica-like plan with aisles divided by lines of pillars, whose central nave stands higher and is illuminated by large windows. The second is a spacious room which opens on to either a garden or the outside view (or both) through doors and windows on all sides, as in the House of the Mosaic Atrium, the House of the Stags and the Hotel House.

The Herculaneum house had many pieces of furniture, but certainly less than we find in our modern dwellings. Among those still preserved to this day, there are several beds, most of which have a high headrest; five little round tables and a crescent-shaped one; fourteen cabinets, four of which are *lararii*; a stool, and a trunk.

Bronze pitcher in the shape of a woman's head, inlaid with silver and copper decorations, a house ornament

Only a few of the beautiful bronze decorations of triclinia, the dining-tables with coaches along three sides, survive. They had to be a rather common piece of furniture in many patrician houses of Herculaneum. We know of many other lost household items, among which there are a number of trunks and chairs, some inlaid. Most of the furniture unearthed is made up of articles akin to those still use in our modern houses. The technical level reached by the craftsmen was very high, as proved by the use of dove-tail joints and of framework panels. Besides various types of wood, master carpenters in Herculaneum used other materials to decorate their furniture. Bronze was often applied, particularly to beds, bone was used for hinges, and glass-pulp for the eye-inlay in the table-leg decorations.

Bronze stool from Herculaneum

VISITING ITINERARY

Admittance to the excavations is currently from the panoramic square at the end of the entrance avenue, lined with cypress trees, over a foot-bridge in the Hotel House at the lower end of the 3rd *cardo* (the first street excavated on the west side). It is hoped, though, that shortly, besides the Antiquarium opening, which is being worked on, there will be a new entrance through a gallery specially excavated in the tuff all the way to the ancient seashore. Here, after seeing the skeletons of the fugitives and admiring the suburban thermal baths, the visitors can walk up to the lower end of the 4th and 5th *cardo* through the ancient slopes and their respective posterns. The buildings along the different sections of the *cardines* are separately described so that the visitor can choose the itinerary they prefer, according to time available. A rather cursory visit requires at least two hours. The visitor can start admiring the view from the upper level, guided by the street plans drawn on a beautiful explanatory ceramic table placed there.

The urban plan

Herculaneum rested on a slightly-sloping, small volcanic plateau which fell sheer to the sea, sided by two deep ravines cut by watercourses, first mentioned in a writing by the ancient historian Sisenna. The city had "safe landing places at any time", that is two inlets, a larger one to the northeast, a smaller to the southwest. Herculaneum was rather small, about 320m wide in the east-west direction, and just a bit more in the north-south direction (up to the rebuilt upper decuman). The area enclosed by the city walls (of which we can see the only side so far exca-vated, the one that lined the high escarpment on the seashore, and which was rebuilt in reticulate masonry in the Augustan age) was of about 20 hectares. Of these, only 4.5 hectares are at the moment visible. Acording to a reliable estimate, at the time of the eruption there was a population of about 4,000 inhabitants.

The city had a rather regular gridlike urban plan, articulated in at least three streets (decumans) in a northwest to southeast direction, inter-sected by five *cardines* perpendicular to both the decumans and the coast-line. An original partition in blocks subdivided into equal rectan-gular lots, based on the Oscan foot measurement, has been recon-noitred. The lower decuman did not have any direct exit to the outside of the city.

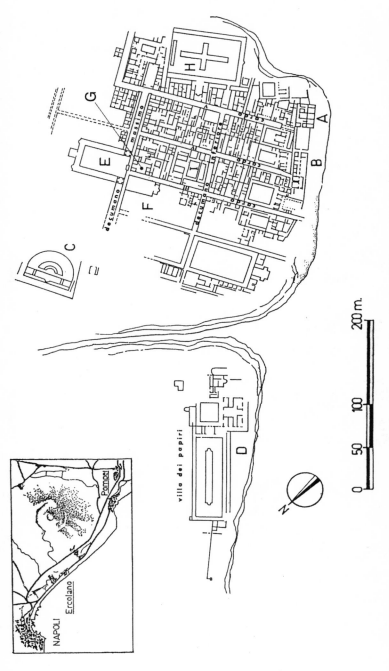

Reconstructed plan of ancient Herculaneum: A) Suburban Thermae; B) Sacred Area; C) Theatre; D) Villa of the Papyri; E) Square (the so-called Basilica); F) Basilica; G) College of the Augustales; H) Palaestra

21

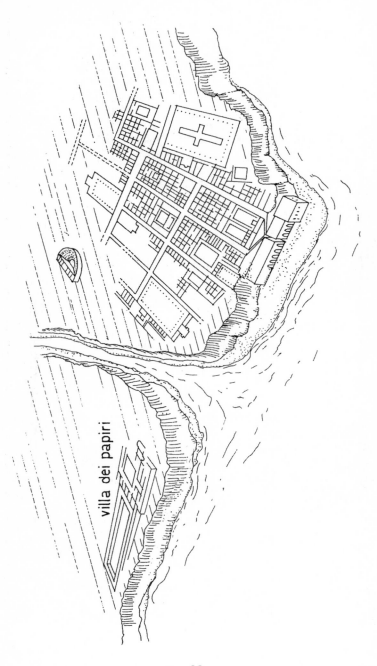

villa dei papiri

Reconstructed elevation of Herculaneum

In the 1st century A.D., when the practical importance of the city walls waned, the more luxurious houses of the urban aristocracy were concentrated, with their terraces, on the cliff overlooking the wonderful Bay of Naples seascape. Starting from the left, we can admire Aristides' House and, following the 3rd *cardo*, the Hotel House; then, beyond the 4th *cardo*, the House of the Mosaic Atrium and the House of the Stags; finally, beyond the 5th *cardo*, the Gemstone House and the really magnificent Telephus' Relief House.

Neo-attic marble relief with Mercury, from a temple in the Sacred Area

Directly on the terrace below, immediately above the seashore and supported by vaulting, there are to the right the Suburban Thermae, an extensive complex whose skylights can be seen from the top, and to the left, a sacred enclosed area, the object of much worship, with two temples side by side, having in front two marble altars. One altar is dedicated to Venus and the other to four deities, as witnessed by the recently discovered wonderful archaic-style reliefs from the Augustan age, originally affixed to the podium of the altar and representing Minerva, Vulcan, Mercury and Neptune (they will be duly exhibited in the Antiquarium; for the time being, casts have been placed in their original site). Both temples were restored after the earthquake of 62 A.D. The pronaos of the first temple was made of fluted and plastered tuff columns, at the moment piled up nearby. The vaulted cell shows remains of frescoes, with garden scenes preceded by transennae painted in reticulate, and a rudder, symbol of the goddess Minerva. The second, larger temple, was endowed with a splendid pronaos paved with rectangular "cipollino" marble slabs, alternatingly smoothed and budded, with columns of the same marble and big Corinthian capitals. A good part of the wooden structure of the roof, which fell down and was dragged to the seashore by the eruption, has been recently recovered. The cell was paved with yellow-marble rhomboid tiles separated by red marble listels. Even the bottom podium, where the aforesaid four reliefs were placed and whose inprints still remain, is clad with marble. The Venusians' College, remembered by an inscription, was nestled in the sacred enclosure. From the first small vaulted room after the entrance to the sacred enclosed area, two frescoes were detached, representing Helen with Paris and a Silenus pouring wine from a vessel in front of the statues of Apollo and Venus. In the second room two statues of togaed acephalic women were discovered; they are currently on view in the Palaestra. In the same place a small altar dedicated to Venus was also hit upon. In the course of removal of pressed-earth paving from the uncovered area in the front, various architectural terracotta pieces were recovered, pertaining to a previous arrangement.

Winged Cupids (tepidarium stucco from the Suburban Thermae)

24

THE ANCIENT SEASHORE
AND THE SUBURBAN THERMAE

More than 250 fugitives ultimately ran towards the seashore and crowded in the arched structures, most of them closed by wooden doors, which were used as storerooms or boat-houses, (except for a few acting as outlets of the city sewer system). The fugitives were found starting from 1981; they were suffocated by the first glowing avalanche to reach Herculaneum, having a temperature in excess of 400 degrees Celsius. Some dogs and two horses were also found. Unlike Pompeii, where plaster casts can be obtained from the hollows left in the ashes by decayed victims' bodies, only their bones are preserved in Herculaneum. But it must be stressed that preservation is generally better here, which is an advantage for the DNA-based studies under way.

When the first group of skeletons was removed, and the difficulty of their *in situ* preservation became evident, a decision was made to leave casts of the skeletons in at least two of the storerooms, with the aim of securing the permanence of the source of the extraordinary emotions

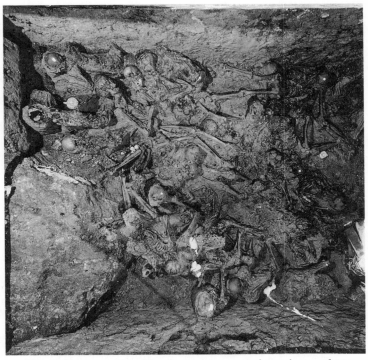

One of the groups of fugitives in a storeroom on the ancient seashore

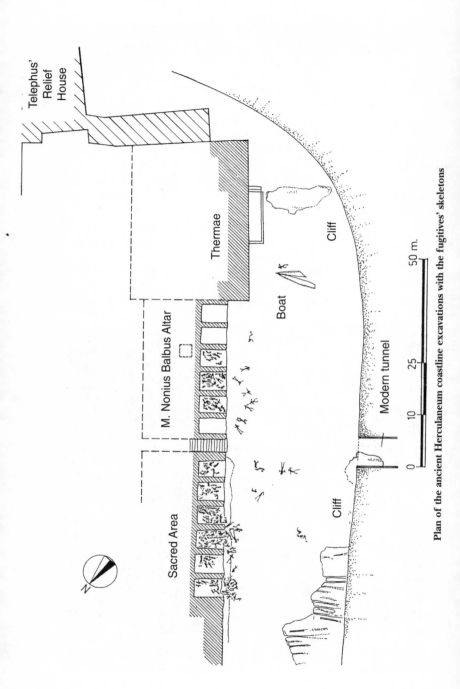

Plan of the ancient Herculaneum coastline excavations with the fugitives' skeletons

Telephus' Relief House

Thermae

M. Nonius Balbus Altar

Sacred Area

Boat

Cliff

Cliff

Modern tunnel

N

0   10   25   50 m.

26

they kindle in the observers — not to mention the pathos arising from presumed family groups. Boundless is the scientific interest provided by the range of studies that can be carried out on this incredible trove of remains of ancient people.

For instance, one of the insights already gained is that the lead concentration in the tissues of a few individuals is at such a level, that it could have created health problems for them. Their muscular and dental conditions are always fine and the diet appears varied, though there are clear distinctions of personal wealth and social status. A fisherman has been recognised on account of deep cuts in his teeth, with which he used to pull-in nets. Plainly moving was the discovery of a pregnant woman, and of great interest that of a soldier with his belt, two gladii, a hammer and several chisels. Among these fugitives, some were attempting to protect themselves with woolen cloth. Scattered among them, several terracotta and bronze oil lamps have been found along with some clay pitchers and little glass vials for ointments. Many of those who were trying to escape carried their most precious belongings with them: house keys, waxed tablets, silverware, splendid gold — and silver jewels, seal rings, a basket of coins, and several little purses — two of them containing a small hoard of gold coins — a wooden money-box with just one coin inside, amulets (among which an Assyrian seal), a little cup of agate. Moreover, some fishing tools were found (a series of hooks and a top), and a box belonging to a physician, with little cylindrical containers for surgical instruments and a small grindstone used to sharpen them.

How massive the burial was, due to the eruption, can be realized by looking at the cliff on the opposite side, where over 20m of volcanic deposits are exposed: six successive pyroclastic flows have been recognised, alternating with six surge deposits, as well as a thin basal layer of pumice fallout.

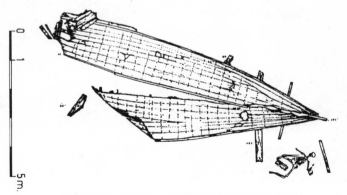

Plant of the boat, as sketched upon its discovery

It is to be remarked that following the Vesuvian coastline sinking, which probably took place at the time of the eruption, the Roman-time seashore is now more than four metres below the present-day sea level. As a consequence it is necessary to keep a pump-system permanently in function which lifts the water to a convenient altitude and directs it, through a tunnel, back to the sea, which is now about 400m distant.

A carbonised, upturned boat about 9m long was found in 1982 on the seashore, right in front of the Suburban Thermae. Its hull is exceptionally well preserved up to the point where the rudder was positioned. The boat was recovered thanks to a complex procedure, and transported inside a pavilion next to the Antiquarium entrance, where its restoration is still under way. Oak wood was used for the planking, walnut for the keel and fir for the fender. The vessel was rapid and light, and was probably navigated by sail and/or with oars and was used for short coastal trade.

After climbing the ancient narrow stairway which leads to the upper terrace, on the right there is the entrance to an enclosure, originally paved with beaten earth, and now with restoration crock, at the centre of which there is a great marble altar, **the cenotaph** of the Augustan period meritorius senator *M. Nonius Balbus*. On its sea-facing side there is the lengthy honorary decree for his municipal senate seat, framed by a festoon embellished with carved Gorgon heads and an outer denticulate motif. The altar was built in the place where his funeral pyre was positioned and the ashes gathered. The honours lavished on him, listed in the decree, were outstanting: an equestrian statue in the Forum, an empty curule chair in the Theatre, an extra day in the athletic games competitions at the Gymnasium in his honour. It was also prescribed

The cenotaph with M. Nonius Balbus' honorary decree

that the cortège during the Ancestors' memorial day should start from this altar.

Behind the altar, on a small marble-clad pedestal, rose the loricate statue of this highly distinguished citizen. According to the inscription it bears, the statue was erected by his freedman *M. Nonius Volusianus.* To this cenotaph also belonged two beautiful torch-bearing sleeping geniuses, acting as acroters of the the square gateway.

From the square **the Suburban Thermae** can be accessed through an entrance marked by two semicolumns supporting a tympanum. The Suburban Thermae were certainly built after a bequest by the same M. Nonius Balbus, who was probably the owner of the overlying luxurious Telephus Relief House and of the Gemstone House partly connected to it. The wall decorations were remade after the 62 A.D. earthquake. On the right there was a small two-roomed tavern, whose walls show several interesting curious drawings, one of which recalls that of a prostitute in the *Vicus Tyanianus* (after Tyana, the main city of Cappadocia) of Pozzuoli, while others show some calculations and a person with a long, dribbling nose. A quantity of building material was deposited nearby at the time of the eruption, evidently for an intended total remake of the wall decorations of the structure. The small room on the left, which Maiuri believed to be a doorkeeper's lodge, was originally a mausoleum with tiny, arched rectangular niches, subsequently incorporated into the thermal baths, bearing witness to the original funerary use of the area. In this same place some tiles were also stocked.

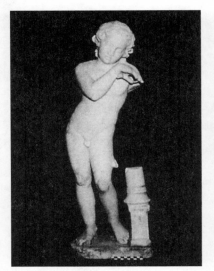

Two sleeping genii belonging to the cenotaph of M. Nonius Balbus

Coming down a stairway whose steps are covered with carbonised wood, now protected by glass panes, one arrives at the well-appointed vestibule, with four columns upon which two series of arches are based, illuminated by a large well of light. The vestibule is enriched by a beautiful marble herma of Apollon, in front of which there is a basin-shaped marble fountain. Worth being noticed is the extraordinary state of preservation of the wooden frames. On the right, through a corridor, there is access to a large, airy entertainment hall with big windows once opening on to the seashore. The flooring of this room is made of terracotta fragments and has for a great part caved in under the weight of volcanic material. A secondary gate leading directly to the seashore can be noticed in the room, as well as various lead pipes. Still on the right, before entering the frigidarium, there is the *praefumium* (oven) with a lead boiler on top, from which hot air and water were sent to the nearby calidarium. The hot air circulated in an interspace below the flooring (hypocaust) which rested on piles of clay tiles, and then upwards

View of the Suburban Thermae frigidarium

behind the walls via terracotta pipes and hollow clay tiles. Hot air and water vapour were conveyed to the vaults, and finally to pipes and chimneys for open-air dispersion.

In the opposite corner there is a service corridor which leads to another *praefumium* and which flanks the walls, thus forming an inner insulation chamber intended to protect the building from moisture. Here, leaning against the wall, some wooden boards and planks are stored.

Through the door in front of the entrance stairway the visitor can enter the frigidarium, a large vaulted room paved with white, rectangular marble slabs, jointed by slate strips and illuminated through a skylight in the ceiling.

One of the tepidarium stucco heroes in the Suburban Thermae, a copy of a classic-age Greek statue

On the west side there is a strip showing traces of extensive repairs, paved with second-hand marble slabs. The walls are decorated with IV style formal architectural motifs. On the right there is a door which gave access to the service side-aisle, still choked with volcanic tuff which filled the room almost to the ceiling. A deep basin lined with pottery fragments is in front of it. On the right, through a wooden door perfectly preserved (it still turns on its hinges) and only partially charred, the visitor can enter the remarkable tepidarium. The floors is paved with rectangular slate slabs separated by strips of lighter-hued marble. On two sides, next to the walls, there are some elegant marble benches, the one under the window with griffin-shaped feet. The walls are coated with white stucco, divided into squares by thin frames with leaf motifs. In the centre of seven of the eight panels thus formed there are seven armed heroes clearly derived from cartoons reproducing classical Greek works. Perhaps they are copies of statues of the "Seven against Thebes" or the seven Epigones dedicated, along Delphi's Sacred Road, to the Argives after a victory on the Spartans in 456 B.C. In the eighth square, lacking a model, there are two little flying Cupids facing each other. Above all of them there is a beautiful white stucco frieze of foliage on a red background. Behind the walls are clay pipes in which hot air coming from the heating furnace used to circulate. The area is illuminated by a rectangular window open on to the sea and surmounted by another smaller window, whose wooden frames are still preserved.

View of the Suburban Thermae calidarium with a marble fountain basin and its imprint in the volcanic tuff (far left)

A small bronze statue with silver and copper agemina from the 17th century excavations

I

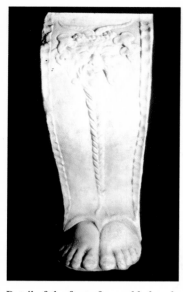

Detail of the foot of a marble bench in the *calidarium* of the ladies' section in the Forum Thermae, showing a head of Pan

Mosaic from the House of the Stags with the head of Ocean

A view of the Palaestra

Vestibule and atrium mosaics from the Atrium House

The *tepidarium* of the Suburban Thermae with stucco decorations in the shape of Greek heroes

Mosaic lararium of the Skeleton House

A view of the *decumanus maximus*

Fresco from the frigidarium dome of the Forum Thermal Baths' male section, showing the fight between a lobster and an octopus, amidst a variety of fish

A view of the College of the Augustales' interior

A fresco in the College of the Augustales while Hercules' introduction to the Olympus

A fresco in the College of the Augustales, with Hercules meeting Acheloo while Deianira, the hero's sweethearth, appearing in the background

A fresco in the cryptoporticus of the Stags House showing a basket full of walnuts, hazelnuts and dates

A view of the 5th lower *cardo* with Neptunis fountain

A painted panel on the decumanus maximus with the Semo Sancus god, wine vases with prices and the announcement of a show in the city of Nola

A round painting in the tablinium of the Bicentenary House portraying a Satyr and a Nymph

Triclinium mosaic of the Neptune and Venus House

Going right through a wooden door, perfectly preserved and by no means seared by the eruption, the vaulted hall of the calidarium is accessed. To the left, a round fountain of "cipollino" marble, located in a wall niche, has a tap in the shape of a wolf's head. The nearby window hosts remnants of double wooden shutters and thick glass panes. At the time of the eruption the fountain, which was used for quick cold ablutions, was pushed forward as the window broke: the basin left a marked cast on the tuff, which includes glass fragments. After the basin was returned to its original position, the cast was left in place undisturbed. The room is paved with marble slabs, and the same material lines the skirting board whose upper edge is finished with a slightly jutting out slate listel. The walls above are splendidly decorated with stucco reliefs — formal architechtural motifs in the IV style (see Appendix no. 2).

Coming out of the calidarium, the door in front provides access to a vast vaulted and apsided hypocaust hall, lavishly paved in marble extending to the lower walls. The stucco coating of the upper walls

Wolf-head shaped tap from the calidarium of the Suburban Thermae

bears formal architectural decorations and a small niche, perhaps containing a deity statuette which hasn't been found. Ample windows open on two sides overlooking the sea, their long lintels reinforced by an iron railing in an amazingly modern structural concept. The centre of the hall is dominated by a large pool heated with the most advanced system of its time, the so-called "samovar" device, consisting of a lead cylinder set in the middle of the pool, accessible from below through a service corridor, in a way that a fire could be started and fed from underneath. This system imparted the water a rather higher temperature compared to that of the simple calidarium pool. Only a few examples of this advanced water-heating system are known (in the Vesuvian area, just one other exists at Stabiae in Villa San Marco) and only that in Herculaneum it is totally preserved. Two small recesses with seats are on the northern side of the hall, and opposite the entrance is the *laconicum* (sauna), round in plan with four small niches facing each other, and

The heathed pool of the Suburban Thermae

with a beautiful mosaic of a black vase against a white background.

Coming out of the Suburban Thermae, up two flights of stairs and two posterns — their hinge holes can be seen, and near one of them some remnants of the door — it is possible to climb to the end of the 4th lower *cardo* (postern on the left) and of the 5th *cardo* (postern on the right). As our guidebook subdivides the visit by sectors, it shall allow visitors to select a preferred itinerary when the new and more convenient access to the excavations will be opened. For the time being our description will have as the starting point the lower end of the 3rd *cardo*, according to the itinerary currently followed.

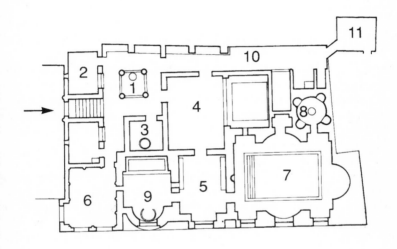

Plan of the Suburban Thermae
1) Anteroom
2) Probable pre-existing mausoleum
3) Furnace
4) Frigidarium
5) Tepidarium
6) Waiting and entertainment room
7) Heathed pool
8) Laconicum
9) Calidarium
10) Service corridor
11) Telephus' Relief House

THE THIRD LOWER *CARDO*

The first house to be visited in the course of this itinerary, is one of the most extensive so far brought to light, the so-called **Hotel House**. Built during the Augustan period, it has a small atrium-lobby on the 4th *cardo* and two service rooms on the 3rd. It seems that when the eruption took place, the house was at least partly in ruin because of the 62 A.D. earthquake. From the atrium, having in its middle a marble-panelled ornamental fountain, one moves to the right directly to the small but well-appointed thermae, the only covered area of the house (ask the custodian to open the door). These facilities, as appropriately described by Petronius, could be used, with permission, even by the landlord's customers. In the calidarium there is a niche ornamented by two black dolphins on a white background, flanking a central palm leaf. The removal of part of the mosaic floor evidences the hollow space underneath, through which hot air was drawn from the furnace to heat the room (hypocaust floor). Left of the atrium, in an area currently closed to the public, there are some living and service rooms with a well-preserved latrine, flushed by water coming from the basin below the impluvium. Hence a ramp goes down to the lower level of the house, where, among other things, there are some rooms finely paved with mosaic and terracotta shards, including a triclinium and a kitchen.

The remainder of the house deployed around a wide peristyle, with a portico paved, on three sides, in white mosaic with a black band. In the adjoining, slightly lower-lying garden, the charred trunk of a pear tree was found. On the northern side of the portico some other rooms, also paved in mosaic and terracotta fragments, are located. On the seaside there is a grandiose banquet hall with a round set of pilasters. The mosaic-floored room beside has a sill decorated with a cock facing another bird. There follows a large living room paved in white mosaic, whose threshold is elegantly finished with black geometric motives within squares.

Left of the exit on the flagstone-paved 3rd *cardo* — the flagstones being cut from gray Vesuvian lava — a tract of the underlying vaulted sewage conduit can be noticed. The sewage system of the city ran in fact beneath each *cardo*, exploiting the marked seaward gradient of the urban area. Connections to the main conduits existed by the houses and public buildings. Further on, a manhole can be recognized in the middle of the same street. On the opposite sidewalk, at no.1 (*hereinafter such numbers refer to the city-plan on p. 8-9*), there is the access to the atrium, paved in pottery fragments flecked with white mosaic tesserae and having in the centre a beautiful limestone fountain, of the so-called

Aristides' House, a name erroneously given after the very famous statue of the orator Eschines, initially believed to be of Aristides, found in the Villa of the Papyri. On two sides of the atrium, the one facing the entrance and the one on the left, there are rows of rooms, while seawards a cliff-edge loggia dominated the panorama. On this side the house rested on massive substructures built in reticulate work and bricks, where a few windows can be seen. On the lower level, reached from the atrium by a small stairway and from the outside through a small chamber which flanks a very steep ramp, there are service rooms with swilling tanks and a room with an oven and a dolium; in this room several skeletons of fugitives were found in the Bourbon era (1734-1861). The partly-vaulted pedestrian ramp, starting from the end of the flagstone-paved street, went all the way down to the seashore.

From a Bourbon-period opening in the wall of the atrium, or from the secondary entrance at no. 2, which is preceded by a portico with pilasters and half-columns, the visitor enters the adjoining **Argus House**, built during the Augustan age, showing a façade in reticulate work, and so far only half-excavated. Its name derives from a small fresco of Argus and Io, now disappeared, that decorated a wide rectangular exedra open on to the spacious peristyle. Beside the exedra is a large hall, frescoed with IV-style fantasy architectural motives on a red background,

The peristyle of the House of Argo, showing the protruding tiles (top left) installed in the course of its restoration

and paved in mosaic. It is now possible to make out only one of its central compositions: a landscape with a charriot, some buildings and three barely-sketched human figures. The other, lost compositions, represented Polyphemus and Galatea, and Hercules in the garden of Hesperides. At the time of excavation of this house (1828) the upper floor, which developed all around the three-sided airy colonnaded peristyle, was found to be in good shape, but after a long discussion involving the then just-established committee for the restoration of Pompeii, and on account of lack of funds, it was decided to preserve only one side of it. The upper floor consisted of several rooms and closets with properly-preserved foodstuff (burlap-packed flour, dried figs wrapped in laurel leaves, walnuts, wheat, prunes, ham) and extended on the 3rd *cardo* sidewalk with a wide gallery supported by lumber beams.

In the Argus House portico, also worth noting is the restoration technique, first applied by F. La Vega in the late decades of the 18th century, which consisted in raising the wall summits to the same level and covering them with roof-tiles projecting from both sides of the wall.

Traces of rectangular paintings removed in the Bourbon era can be noticed on the peristyle walls.

From the large perystile the visitor can access a second, smaller one, which has fluted, stuccoed columns linked together by a low wall with vestiges of garden-paintings, partly visible through Bourbon-era tunnels. To the left there are two small chambers, paved in mosaic, a cubicle (sleeping room) with traces of the bed recess, and a small sitting room. Further ahead, along the escarpment, the fragment of a beautiful black-and-white mosaic with various decorations such as swastikas and amazon shields, commands attention. Looking upwards, the painted, partly collapsed ceiling, with remnants of its lathwork, can also be noticed.

Other gracefully frescoed and mosaic-paved rooms are on the seaward side — some of them were being decorated at the time of the eruption — facing an as-yet unexcavated atrium, along with an ample hall opening on to a panoramic terrace, adorned with IV style frescoes. Two painting are in the centre, one showing Dirce's supplice (on the background is the fortified city of Thebes, and a man bearing a rod on his shoulder is seen coming out of one of its doors), the other showing Perseus, wearing Pluto's helmet and helped by Minerva, in the act of cutting the head of Medusa. From the terrace a set of steps leads down to a few small chambers at a lower level, including a vaulted sacellum equipped with a podium. Along the way down is the only known tract of the pre-Roman fortification, a course of mortarless squared tuff blocks.

Proceding along the 3rd *cardo*, to the left, at no.3 (*ins.* II), is the porticoed back entrance, furnished with a spacious vestibule and a porter's lodge, of the **House of the Genius**, a name deriving from a lost fresco in the corner pilaster of the peristyle, also only partly excavated. The peristyle itself, stylish and breezy, is paved with terracotta shards and mosaic. In the middle of the garden, surrounded by a colonnaded portico, there is a marble-lined rectangular basin, with niches in the corners.

Still further ahead, on the opposite sidewalk, at no.3 of the *ins.* III, opens the **House of the Skeleton**, so called after the upper-floor discovery, during the Bourbon era, of a skeleton flanked by two seats. It is to be remarked that above this house, and the two described immediately before, poor, late-ancient (i.e. post-79 A.D.) tombs were discovered. Even though the House of the Skeleton is not particularly large, it shows important decorations. A long corridor, skirting the porter's lodge, brings to a spacious forecourt, recently re-paved with terracotta fragments: it was originally paved in black mosaic bordered by a white band. To the right is a cubicle, while frontally opens a small but refined tablinum, once floored with marble slabs as revealed by their imprints and by the few remaining ones. The parietal decoration is in the IV style, with fantasy architectural motives on a red background. To the left lies instead a wide triclinium, paved in white mosaic bordered by a black band, siding a nymphaeum ornamented with a marble fountain. Its back wall is covered with scoriaceous lava fragments flecked with seashells, and with a beautiful mosaic frieze. On the left two panels remain, one with a young shepherd leading a ram to sacrifice, the other with a drinking horn suspended from a ribbon. Another panel is at the far right of the frieze, showing an offerer with a doe. The big mosaic-covered central niche and the other panels of the frieze were cut and taken away in 1740. They are now in the National Archaeological Museum in Naples: we have had the cast executed and put back in place, as a part of a wider program of studies and actions aiming at offering the public a better grasp and understanding of the Herculanean monuments. In the central part of the frieze there was a panel with a reclining Bacchus and a panther, while two side-panels had Tritons and garlands.

Back to the atrium, a corridor on the tablinum side reaches a large apsided hall, paved with marble and painted with IV-style architectural motives, open to a tiny courtyard enhanced by a lararium with mosaics and seashells among garden pictures. A small marble panel, with a flying Cupid holding a money purse, is set in the wall. The courtyard was closed high up by an iron grille, still partly preserved.

Walking back once more to the atrium, another corridor to the left leads to the rest of the house, perhaps a later addition. Worth noticing here is a mosaic-covered daytime cubicle, illuminated from a small courtyard, with the bed standing on a low platform, and two other elegantly frescoed cubicles at the back of it.

Getting out of the House of the Skeleton, after a few steps the visitor is at the intersection with the lower decuman. To the left there is **a bar** (*thermopolium*): its marble-lined counter includes the usual large clay vessels (*dolii*) for food and drinks. Their round lids have been removed and set aside for security reasons. To the right is another **shop**, connected to the House of the Wooden Partition, preserving an interred broken dolium repaired with lead braces. In this place, in the words of the excavations journal, "a terracotta fragment containing a quantity of fish scales and fishbones was found". In the nearby shops along the decuman a large amount of carbonized wheat was collected.

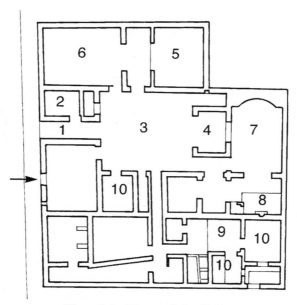

Plan of the House of the Skeleton
1) Anteroom
2) Porter's lodge
3) Atrium
4) Tablinum
5) Nimphaeum with the cast of the mosaic- ornamented niche
6) Triclinium
7) Living room
8) Courtyard with lararium
9) Daytime bedroom
10) Bedrooms

THE THIRD UPPER *CARDO*
AND THE LOWER DECUMAN

After crossing the lower decuman, there is a shop on the left (*ins.* VII, no.1), annexed to a small house accessible from the same street. In the niche of the courtyard there stood a small altar in dark-hued marble, bearing a consecration epigraph to the goddess *Salus*. We know that the house belonged to a certain *C. Messenius Eunomus* (also recorded in a graffito on a column of the College of the Augustales) from a bronze seal, discovered alongside two gold rings, three gemstones and a few little silver spoons.

At no.2 there is the back entrance to the **House of Galba** (only half-excavated and currently closed to the public), which is one of the oldest residences, preserving a good deal of the original end-of-the-2nd / beginning-of-the-1st century B.C. plan. The house derives its name from the discovery (in the street outside) of a small, rare silver bust — now in the National Archaeological Museum in Naples — of the emperor who overthrew Nero. Through a corridor, flanked by a small janitor's room and a kitchen with adjoining latrine, a peristyle is approached, whose fluted grey-tuff columns were at a later stage covered with red stucco. On the left-hand side originally there was a double colonnade, but one line of columns was later incorporated into a row of cubicles. In the centre of the peristyle is a marble-clad, cross-shaped fountain. On the eastern side there is an elegant rectangular room floored with terracotta shards which looks on to the courtyard. The walls of the room are imaginatively decorated with architectural motifs painted in the IV style.

Back in the street, while on the left just the façades of a row of shops and houses have been exposed, on the right a passageway leads to the Palestra and the small arched entrance to the male section of the **Forum Thermae**. Beside the passageway is a rather well-preserved **public latrine**, paved with bricks arranged in herringbone pattern. The flush is cut from vesuvian stone and the sewage channel, once surmounted by rows of adroitly-shaped marble seats removed in the Bourbon era, is lined with tiles.

The Forum Thermae probably date back to Caesar's epoch, and were originally fed from a large waterwell, whose bronze water-lifting wheels have been found and will be placed in the room at the corner between the lower *decumanus* and the 4th *cardo*. Only at a later stage, following the construction of the Augustan Serino aqueduct did the Thermae receive an adequate water supply, but the old device wasn't totally discarded. The outer walls are built in *opus reticulatum,* the remainder in *opus incertum.* The Thermae were quite well-attended, because there were few citizens who could afford the luxury of adequate bathing facilities in their own homes. If the Thermae, unlike the case in point, didn't have separate symmetrical ladies and gentlemen sections, access, at a reasonable cost, was at different times for each sex.

The vestibule (*apodypterium*) is a rectangular ante-room paved with stone fragments laid in the mortar bed; at one side is a niche with a fountain and a marble basin for preliminary ablutions; all around are masonry seats and stalls. The barrel vault, like others in similar rooms, is scored by a series of parallel grooves, meant not only as aestehtic motives but above all as a way of trapping hot air in the room for as long as possible. Here, in the course of excavations, three clustered skeletons were discovered, coins and precious objects lying beside them. The skeletons belonged to fugitives who had hoped to find shelter under the vaulted structures of the building — which as a matter of fact withstood the blast of several pyroclastic flows very well. To the left a small passage provides access to the circular *frigidarium,* ornamented with four yellow-coloured niches, a blue-coloured pool, red walls decorated with chandeliers, and an azure vaulted ceiling displaying lively fish and other marine life. The place is lighted through a round opening in the summit of the dome. Back to the entrance room, the visitor, through a little arched door, can enter the *tepidarium,* heated by hot air circulating under the raised floor, which is paved in white mosaic; in the middle is

Floor mosaic with a Triton among dolphins, in the tepidarium of the Forum Thermae

a black double-frame enclosing a triton and four dolphins. Next is the *calidarium*, where the vault has almost entirely collapsed, exposing to view the hot-vapour exhaust pipes and smoke chimneys that flanked it. On the southern side is a large niche with the masonry base of a marble fountain *(labrum)* used for speedy cold-water ablutions, removed in the Bourbon era. On the opposite side is the marble-clad rectangular pool.

Once out of the male section of the thermal facilities, the ample Palaestra can be visited, which is surrounded by a colonnaded portico paved with terracotta fragments and graced by elegant architectural motifs, frescoed in the IV style on a black and white background, well-preserved in a corner. On the southern side of the peristyle there are some rooms of uncertain purpose, but they were probably somehow related to the exercises taking place in the adjoining open area.

Back to the 3rd *cardo* and proceeding beyond the above-mentioned latrine, a large, window-like opening comes to the visitor's attention, perhaps pertaining to an ancient public waterwell. Next is a workshop

The kitchen of the House of the Two Atria

(*ins.* VI, no.29) equipped with an oven and a large clay vessel — probably a dye-works — and then the beautiful façade of the **House of the Two Atria** can be admired. The striking prospect is made up of two floors in *opus reticulatum* separated by a moulding. A gorgon mask on the keystone of the gate had the task of keeping the evil-eye at bay. Worth noticing are small windows on the façade, one of them still protected by its original iron grille. Through the large door, overlain by a moulded cornice cut from tuff blocks, the visitor enters the first atrium, paved with terracotta fragments interspersed with marble flakes, its central basin surrounded by four columns supporting the roof. To the left is a small kitchen equipped with an oven, a latrine and large water vessels, all in a good state of presevation. From a small room to the right of the entrance a wooden stair led to the upper floor which extended all over the house. A gallery surrounding this first atrium connected the two sections of the upper storey. The *tablinum* provides access to the second, smaller atrium, carrying a rectangular impluvium that fed rainwater to the underlying cistern, whose opening was also used to draw water for the household needs. From the atrium, through a small vestibule and its marble threshold, a small living room was reached: here a large window, opening on to the atrium, illuminated gorgeous frescoes with IV style architectural decorations, displaying blue-backed pavilions. At the far end of the atrium is a large triclinium, flanked by two. service rooms. A small archive of 20 tablets, found in a wooden casket in the room north of the *tablinum,* probably belonged, by exclusion, to a certain *Herennia Tertia.*

Still to the left, the secondary entrance of the great **House of the Tuscan Colonnade** follows (no.26) and then the side entrance of the **College of the Augustales** (no.24). This is a fine rectangular hall, whose peripheral walls, built in reticulate work with squared tuff blocks braced by clay bricks, adjoin to the inside a set of arches supported by pilaster strips. Four columns rising in the interior bear, by the means of four charred beams — still partly preserved — a raised central body, through which plenty of daylight entered the hall. The flooring is in terracotta shards and the walls are painted black in the lower part, while in the upper part the white plaster remains exposed. A fallen inscribed plaque, once affixed to the wall but found under the raised central body, records that the building, dedicated to the emperor of that time, Augustus, was erected by two brothers, *A. Lucius Proculus* and *A. Lucius Iulianus,* who on inauguration day offered a lunch party to the members of the municipal senate and to the Augustales. The latter was a class somewhat in between the decurions and the commoners, therefore expressing a desirable social status, made up principally of rich freedmen (in Herculaneum a whole century was composed of freedmen).

What have been thought so far to be the College rosters, found in fragments to the north of the building near the Basilica entrance, according to recent studies and based on their large numbers, could instead refer to another college, or be the list of the free citizens. Resting on bases leaning against the two columns near the main entrance — as stated by inscriptions removed in the 18th century — were the statues of deified Julius Caesar and Augustus. One of the columns is inscribed with propaganda graffiti relating to the College cooptation (the College house is indicated as *Curia Augustana*). To the right of the entrance a small gatekeeper's lodge was obtained by erecting a masonry panel. Here the guardian was found dead in his own bed, which is now on view. The long charred pole, also visible, prodded up an unstable section of the ceiling. In the far-end area of the hall two partition walls abutting against the shafts of two columns — elegantly painted as palm-tree trunks — defined a gorgeous raised (by two steps) sacellum, paved with high-quality marble slabs extending to the skirting boards, and decorated with parietal architectural motives in the IV style. On the side walls are two beautiful central paintings: the one to the left hints at Hercules' introduction to the Olympus, with Minerva, Juno and Jupiter in the shape of a rainbow; the opposite one hints at Hercules' struggle with the river Acheloo, shown as a man with a fluvial deity's horns, who had seized and was keeping hostage Hercules' beloved Deianira. Both paintings derive from splendid Hellenistic originals.

A statue pedestal, dominated by a laurel crown painted above, lies against the end-wall of the hall. The crown is a reminder of that decreed by the community of Herculaneum in honour of Augustus and the empire. The building was criss-crossed by Bourbon tunnels, traces of which are still clearly identifiable, and in due time the diggers took away part of the sacellum marble décor.

In front of the side entrance to the College the surrounding wall of **the Civic Basilica**, with two side-entrances to the same, can be seen. The Basilica was built in the Augustan period by M. Nonius Balbus and was restored after the earthquake of 62 AD, when it was re-painted with IV style ornaments, including a frieze of Hercules' minor endeavours with Greek inscriptions. The Civic Basilica was a rectangular body measuring 16.5x29 metres and opening on to the *decumanus maximus* with a large central gateway. Its interior had two orders of fluted and stuccoed semi-columns, the lower one in the Ionian and the upper one in the Corinthian style (just a little more than 12 metres in height) supporting wooden trusses. A few of the fine stuccoed-tuff capitals can still be admired. Positioned against the walls there were statues of M. Nonius Balbus' family members. The building ends with a large exedra that can be now accessed via a Bourbon tunnel.

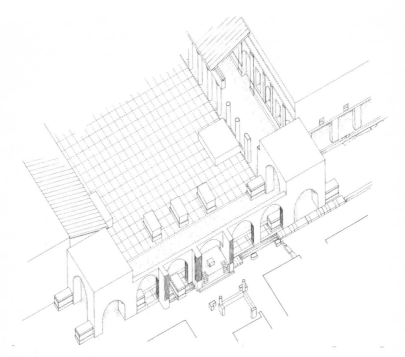

Elevation of the entrance area to the porticoed square of the so-called Basilica

The four-sided arch of the "Basilica" with the pedestals of two equestrian statues

The College of the Augustales faced northwards a spacious porticoed piazza with niches and an end-side sacellum, where the statue of the emperor Titus, who reigned at the time of the eruption, was discovered, along with those probably belonging (no heads were found when they were dug out) to Vespasian and Augustus, deified and seated in heroic nakedness. The piazza, built in 49 A.D. and restored by Vespasian after the 62 A.D. earthquake, was accessible laterally through a couple of monumental four-sided arches. The one at the front of the Civic Basilica entrance flaunts a bronze quadriga mounted by the emperor Claudius, also portrayed in heroic nakedness. The side porticoes ended in two ample exedrae: from their walls famous frescoes were detached showing Hercules and Telephus, Theseus and the Minotaur, Kyron and Achilles, Pan and Olympus — now prominently displayed in the National Archaeological Museum in Naples. Before these exedrae, at the intersection with the arms of the colonnade, there were the bronze statues of Augustus and Claudius, again in heroic nakedness. The side niches, alternatingly plain- and round-bottomed, hosted bronze statues of other members of the imperial family. Recovered in Bourbon times were those of Tiberius, Livia, and another woman with the attributes of an Isis' priestess, probably Flavia Domitilla. Only the inscriptions of other statues have been found. All of them were removed in due time to the aforesaid museum. Just the southern end of the piazza, paved in

A round marble-relief with Achilles interrogating the oracle, from the entrance of the Civic Basilica

marble slabs, and with the pertaining four-sided monumental arch, has so far been excavated. A series of pedestals for equestrian statues can be seen, and two other bases lying against the marble-clad pilasters of the southern portico; one of them once bearing, as attested by the relevant inscription, the statue of Iulia, Titus' daughter. The intrados of the arcades of the southern portico was decorated with large flower-shaped stuccoes, identical to those in the four-sided arches. In the western part, the arcaded pilasters of the portico were at a certain point in time connected through partition walls to the previous portico, whose brick columns, being absorbed into the walls, were thus transformed into half-columns, while on the eastern side, where the span between pilasters and columns was wider, it was preferred to renounce such structural connection. The reason behind this course of action remains unknown, but it is possible to speculate that, due to the fact that it was difficult, in the Claudian age, to carve out the necessary space for such an extensive piazza, some of the extant features had to be left standing. To the side of the main entrance to the College of the Augustales there

Screw-press for clothes, from a shop on the lower decuman

48

is what might amount to a triclinium (but some believe it to be a public latrine or a sacellum) open to the air in the upper part of the walls by the means of thin marble colonnettes adorned with intricate Corinthian capitals, and having in front of it a marble-clad podium accessible through a short flight of steps. Nearby, in the corner of one of the brick pilasters, the white plaster bears the graffito of a ship, its big sail unfurled to the wind. Another podium closes the 3rd *cardo* on the side of the piazza. To the right of the main entrance to the College of the Augustales a small, rectangular sacellum opens, faced with rich marble and having a podium in the back wall, followed by a *thermopolium* (bar) with masonry counters and large *dolii*, criss-crossed by Bourbon era tunnels. At present part of this area is closed to the public due to the risk of collapse of the overlying escarpment.

Out of the College and back to the lower decuman — a street once jammed with traffic, as attested by the well-marked ruts cut into the flag-stones by the wheels of the carts — the visitor turns left and, skirting the Forum Thermae perimetral wall, reaches the intersection with the 4th *cardo*. On the left, in a small place connected with the palaestra of the Thermae, an exhibition will be set up on this bathing establishment and on the Herculaneum water supply, where the original water-lifting device of the already mentioned waterwell, located north of the building complex, will be shown.

On the opposite side, at no.10, there is a shop with the only surviving specimen of **a wooden screw-press for clothes**, now in the National Archaeological Museum in Naples (inventory no.9774), also depicted in a Pompeii fresco. The trading establishment included tiny living quarters for the owner, made up of two rooms on the upper floor, accessible through a flight of timber steps. Here a window opens on to the atrium of the House of the Wooden Partition, indicating that the shop-keeper somehow must have been connected with the owner of the house.

At the opposite corner of the intersection a square masonry pillar can be observed, one of the *castella aquaria* connected to a branch of the Augustan aqueduct of Serino that provided a convenient, abundant water supply for the city. The *castella* regulated the water distribution and kept the pressure in the pipe system at an adequate level. Water was raised to a tank resting on the top of the pillar, whence it was conveyed to a network of lead pipes of various sizes.

THE FOURTH LOWER *CARDO*

Once the visitor turns right along the 4th lower *cardo*, he is in front of the **Wooden Partition House** façade, covered with white plaster and perfectly preserved up to its eaves (*ins.* III, no.11). Note the small windows which are typical nowadays of oriental houses; in fact most of the air and light used to get in through the atrium opening and the airy internal courtyards. Through the large door flanked by big tuff blocks, overlain by a decorated frame and having at its sides two brick benches, the visitor can approach the access corridor paved with terracotta fragments and decorative insets of white mosaic tesserae. The corridor, past the porter's room on the left, leads to the large atrium, well-preserved and similarly paved, whose walls are elegantly frescoed with architectural IV style formal decorations on a red and black background. In the centre there is the impluvium, the marble basin collecting rainwater and sending it to the nearby cistern. The mouth of the cistern, whence water was drawn, can also be observed. In its original state, as it appears through the partly missing bottom marble slabs, the basin was lined with terracotta fragments and geometrical mosaic listels as decorations.

Beside the basin there was a marble desk decorated with lion heads.

The atrium is closed, on the tablinum side, by a large wooden parti-

View of the 4th lower cardo

tion decorated with bronze studs, two of which shaped, as in Trimalchion House, like the prow of a ship. The partition, whence the house gets its name, rises one third the height of the room. On the right of the entrance aisle there is a large bedroom (*cubiculum*), lit by a small window open to the street. The bedroom is paved with black and white mosaic, consisting of orthogonal partitions and lozanges, crossed by diagonal lines. In this area a small marble desk was found, its support fashioned after a statue of the deity Attis wearing his typical Phrygian cap. On the left there are two other bedrooms, in one of which the carbonised bed, left in place, was found. The tablinum pavement is in white mosaic, and its threshold is decorated with a long ivy branch wrapped around a pole; the ornamental paintings of the walls spread on a black background, with the remains of a small central picture of a theatre mask. On the side of the garden the area was closed by a large wooden door, as indicated by the hinge holes. On the left of the tablinum there is a large dining-room, also connected to the peristyle quarter through a door, and paved with terracotta fragments and white mosaic. The elegant fresco decoration of the room, on a red background, is mostly preserved, and on the northern side the central picture of a pastoral-idyllic scene (a landscape with a small prominent temple, and some female figures) can be seen. From this hall or from the tablinum the visitor can walk to the peristyle quarter, with a colonnade of pillars and semi-columns surrounding the garden on three sides (the fourth side shows a baseboard decorated with garden drawings, and an upper colonnaded loggia, perhaps built just for a scenic effect; visitors can ask the attendant to have access here). On the northern side there are two bedrooms, one paved with mosaic, the other with terracotta fragments, both showing on the walls remains of fresco decorations; a skeleton was found in one of them. On the west side there is a large triclinium and another bedroom in which there was a painting of Mars and Venus. A passage room, where there is the kitchen and the latrine on the right side, led to the already-described foodshop on the corner between the 3rd *cardo* and the lower decuman, run by the owner of the house.

Once out of the Wooden Partition House and turning right, preceded by a portico with its loggia overhanging the street, the visitor can see one of the most singular building complexes in Herculaneum — actually including a total of five small apartments — that is the **Trellis House** (*ins.* III, no.13-15). The trellis work, described by Vitruvius (who, because of the fire-danger it poses, preferred it had never been invented) was a wall structure which gained much appreciation during the Mediaeval age and is still used in the East: it is made up of wooden frames intertwined with stone squares and cementing material.

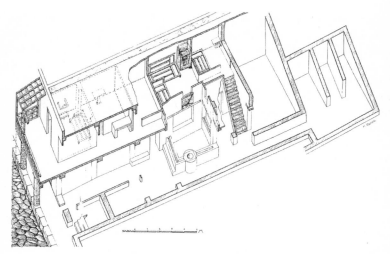

Trellis House elevation (*from Maiuri, 1958*)

Sometimes, as in the courtyard, lathwork was used, which provided light to the rooms nearby through spacious windows. The wooden winch and rope, used to draw water from the cistern, is perfectly preserved and displayed in a showcase along the street.

Two sets of stairs lead to the upper level, one from the street (no.13), the other from the courtyard. In three different rooms of the two small

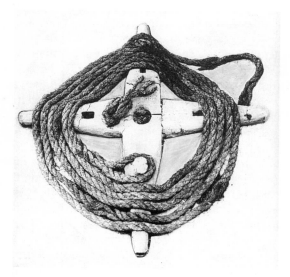

Wooden winch and charred rope from the Trellis House courtyard

upper-floor apartments — one of which, supported by three brick columns, overhung the sidewalk — a total of five carbonized beds, still on the spot, two wardrobes and a lararium were found, as well as a series of bronze statues and a wooden one, which is very interesting on account of its rarity.

Once out of the Trellis House and proceeding straight on, upon reaching no.16, there is the small **Bronze Herm House** to the right, with a Tuscan atrium paved with potsherds and including a central tuff basin. The wall drawings in the IV style are of the candelabra type. A cast of the bronze herm — a portrait of the house owner — is exhibited here. On the street side of the atrium lies a cubicle, and in front of it there is the tablinum (floored with coloured stone slabs and small fragments of marble laid out in lime), a simple, undecorated room with a well and a long corridor which leads to a small room behind the tablinum and to a large triclinium. In the latter the central drawings were renewed during the IV style times. The better-preserved one is a marine landscape.

At no.17 the visitor can see the narrow rectangular **Brick Altar House,** one of the smaller Herculaneum houses, preserving the dimensions of one of the original lots of the Oscan urban plan. The façade, covered with a long wooden shed, has a baseboard decorated in white stucco with black oblique bands. A large inscription in red letters is above it. At the end of the courtyard on the far side of the house, next to the wall, in an area once probably sheltered by a roof, there is, on a lower level, a large brick altar, which was the domestic lararium.

Wooden head from the Trellis House

Once out of the house, crossing to the opposite sidewalk, the visitor reaches the entrance to one of the richest Herculaneum dwellings, the **House of the Mosaic Atrium** (*ins.* IV, no.2). Since the atrium is unstable, the peristyle quarter can be currently accessed through the secondary entrance at no.1. The vestibule pavement is in black and white mosaic shaped as large squares separated by plaited bands and decorated with various geometric motifs. On the left is the doorkeeper's room, while the kitchen is on the right, with an entrance also from the atrium.

The large Tuscan atrium has a marble basin in its centre, and is

Atrium of from the House of the Mosaic Atrium (photo courtesy of Linda Butler)

paved with black and white mosaic in a chessboard pattern. A garland-ed band surrounds the basin. Note how distorted this band is, due both to incorrect squaring of the floor surface and to its undulation, a result of poor compaction of the underlying earthen bed, which probably yielded under the weight of the volcanic material that piled up on top of it during the eruption. At the back of the atrium, instead of a tablinum, there is a large monumental basilica-like hall, divided into three aisles by two lines of three rectangular pillars. This matches per-fectly Vitruvius' description of one of the architectural innovations of his time, the "Egyptian Hall" (*oecus aegyptius*). The central nave, sur-mounted by wooden trusses, is higher and lit by two windows on each side. The floor is made up of precious marble slabs while the wall dec-oration, very elegant in its animal and vegetal motives, is on a white background and in the IV style.

The large garden is surrounded by a windowed cryptoporticus, part-ly consisting of a verandah with glass panes in a wood framing, still most-ly preserved. The garden has a rectangular marble fountain basin, and a marble-paved exedra with frescoes on a light-blue background. Two central drawings depict on the left Dirce's torture and on the right Diana bathing naked, with Atteon, who was staring at her, torn to pieces by dogs. On the two sides of the exedra there are other areas paved with mosaics and elegantly frescoed, among which a remarkable red cubicle whose painted ceiling is still preserved. On the seaward side there is a large hall richly paved with marble, and some finely decorated rooms. Among them is a particularly striking one, painted white, with a pretty

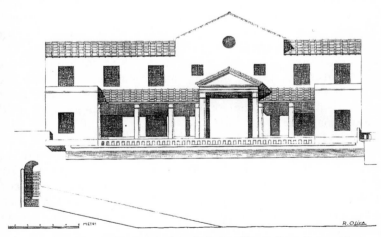

Southern prospect of the Mosaic Atrium House, from the seaside, with the little door on the IV *cardo* (after Maiuri, 1958)

sacral-idyllic landscape, drawn on a partition, of a horseman riding towards a rustic sacellum in the shape of a small aedicula among trees and rocks. Another horseman appears in perspective on the background. The rooms face a colonnaded portico paved with black mosaic and marble chips, once open to the sea view. At the extremities of the portico there are two diurnal cubicles with black and white marble flooring, particularly suited to peaceful enjoyment of the delightful view and the mildness of the weather.

Out of the House of the Mosaic Atrium and walking up to the right, at no.4, between two brick benches, there is the entrance to the **Alcove House**, with a well-preserved reticulate façade. At no.3 a stairway, partly masonry, partly wood, led to the upper storey. The house results from joining two independent, long, narrow units. The entry corridor leads to a vestibule opening on to a courtyard with a rectangular exedra. Beyond the courtyard, there is a little hall on the left where the visitor can see the only drawing that escaped the attention of the Bourbon excavators, showing a forsaken Ariadne and Theseus' ship departing. Further on, around another little courtyard, there are various bedrooms and service rooms, and a triclinium. Returning to the vestibule and going down two steps, there is a second, larger vestibule paved in black mosaic with coloured marble chips. This vestibule opens, on one side, on to a marble floored *biclinium* with elegant frescoed IV-style wall decorations and well-preserved wooden beds; on the other side there is a large dining hall with a few remnants of a rich marble flooring. On its side a long corridor paved in mosaic, skirting a small courtyard, leads, past a vestibule, to an isolated alcove in the shape of an apsed hall, adorned with simple linear decorations on the walls and the ceiling.

Back to the entrance and turning right, at no.6 is the entrance to the **Fullonica House**, developing around two small, subsequent atria. The first atrium was used as a *fullonica* (laundry) due to the installation of two washbasins. The second one has an impluvium lined with potsherds, and dates back to at least to the 2nd century B.C., as in the two end-areas it is possible to notice the remains of decoration in marble-like stucco squares in relief (I style).

Out of the Fullonica House, turning right, at no.8, there is the small **Painted Papyrus House**, so called for a small painting drawn above the entrance to the little courtyard, depicting two inkpots and a papyrus scroll with a Greek inscription, unfortunately lost soon after its discovery. However the visitor can see an interesting graffito on a red background protected by glass, which recalls the Herculaneum ship-owners' activity in connection with the port of Pozzuoli.

THE FOURTH UPPER *CARDO*

Once back at the intersection with the lower decuman and having left it behind, the visitor will see, immediately on his right, one of the best preserved and most ancient Herculaneum houses (2nd century B.C.), the **Samnite House** (*ins.* V, no.1). Originally it covered the entire block, but in the back garden area two other houses were later inserted. The beautiful façade, remade in reticulate work during the Augustan age, still shows the large original entrance doorway, cut from tuff, with beautiful Corinthian capitals. The vestibule has a I style Pompeiian decoration imitating variously-coloured marble blocks. On one of them there is a small name inscription in Oscan lettering. Above the stucco dentelled frame there is a band with a landscape, while the ceiling presents painted caissons. Maiuri thought it to be a later addition, while more recent research considers it synchronous with the decoration. The atrium has a central marble-clad basin and the original flooring is in terracotta fragments with interspersed white mosaic chips. Note, on the top, the roof-gutter tiles with wolf-head protomos. The atrium decoration was redone in the lower part with IV-style formal architectural motifs, while in the upper area, over a moulded stucco frame, a false

View of the trompe l'oeil upper gallery of the Samnite House atrium

57

open gallery unwinds, open on the eastern side with Ionic semicolumns and closed in the lower part by reticulate transennae.

On the right of the entrance vestibule there is a bedroom with a wall decoration in delicate monochrome on an aquamarine-green background with tenuous shadings: it shows light architectural aediculae and a central drawing of the rape of Europa. On the left there is another area with late II-style decoration on a white background. Note the strange graffiti beside the entrance, among which it is possible to recognize a strange winged Genius holding a whip, a cock and an antelope. On the left there are two cubicles and the stairway which gives access to the upper level. The tablinum shows a wonderful flooring in terracotta fragments decorated with white mosaic: a winding band surrounded by reticulate work, and a central medallion divided into rhombs, with four small palm trees between two dolphins in the corners. The wall decoration is on a red background, which in some areas has turned yellow due to the high temperature at the time of burial by the eruption. The little hall next to the tablinum presents a nice wall decoration of aediculae on a cerulean background.

As the visitor exits the Samnite House and proceeds to the right, he will find at no. 3-4 (*ins.* V) the **Loom House**. The name of its last two owners is known thanks to a marble plate inscribed on both sides, mentioning a certain *Iulia* and an *M. Nonius Dama* (a cast is exposed along the street). The house, with a rather unrefined appearance, has only a few small rooms around an arcaded courtyard (where a nice camphor tree has been planted). The premises next to the street was a real weaving workshop.

In front of the Loom House there is the entrance to the **women's section of the Forum Thermal Baths** (*ins.* VI, no.8). From a living room paved and covered with terracotta fragments with benches along the walls, the visitor can enter the vestibule (*apodyterium*) through a small arched door. On the left there is a corridor, once paved with marble slabs (only their imprints remain) which led to the gymnasium of the Thermal Baths through a small arched door, later closed. The corridor was thus transformed into the porter's room. Note that the entrance to the vestibule of the women's Thermal Baths was originally through the small but well decorated entrance at no. 9, paved with black mosaic and marble chips, preceded by a small porch, itself accessible through a little arched door which also was closed later .

The *apodyterium*, perfectly preserved, is a room with a curry-combed barrel vault. All around the walls there is a brick bench overlain by some stalls used for clothes. The flooring is in black and white mosaic representing a rudder-handling Triton (a mythologic being, part of Neptune's retinue) whiplashed by a winged Cupid and surrounded by four dolphins, an octopus and a cuttle-fish. The room was lit through a small round hole protected by a glass pane.

A little arched door leads to the tepidarium, which has a similar conformation, with wall benches and black and white mosaic flooring of labyrinthine motifs including little objects (amphora, trident, phallus, etc.). Through another small door the larger, similarly vaulted calidarium can be accessed.

Vestibule of the women's section in the Forum Thermal Baths: the mosaic depicts a helm-handling Triton among marine animals

On the left, in the apse-shaped niche there is a brick shelf upon which a marble-basin fountain (*labrum*) used for quick cold-water ablutions was placed, only to be removed during the Bourbon age. In front there is a rectangular marble bath. The flooring is in white mosaic framed by a black band. In a gap in the floor, protected by an iron grating, the hypocaust structure is clearly visible, as well as the clay pipes in the walls for hot-air circulation. Two benches, one made of white marble resting on feet elegantly decorated with Pan heads, the other made of red marble with gryphon-shaped feet, are a special feature of the room.

Leaving the Thermal Baths and crossing to the opposite sidewalk, at no. 5 (*ins.* V), the entrance to the **House of the Charred Furniture**, at present closed to the public, can be noticed. The house shows a traditional layout consisting of a vestibule, an atrium with a small bath, a tablinum, an upper-level apartment open towards the atrium through a colonnaded arcade, and a garden. The house was partly redecorated in the late III style during the Claudian age. On the street side, all around the atrium, there is a triclinium, paved in white mosaic exhibiting a central square of polychrome marble and a rich attractive architectural decoration painted in the IV style, and an alcove. At the back of the garden, aligned with the house entrance, there is an altar (lararium) in the form of a little prostyle temple with an oyster-like stucco niche. A triclinium, with a beautiful architectural red monochromic wall decoration above a black baseboard, opens on to the garden: inside, a veneered bed with high sides and back was found, along with a small kitchen table with feet in the shape of greyhound protomes.

Exiting the house and continuing to the right, at no.6 there is an interesting **foodshop**, connected at the back with the House of Neptune and Amphitrytes. Thanks to the collapse of the ceiling, the visitor can see the kitchen and some of the upper-level rooms, where the bronze leg of a bed is on view. Well preserved is a carbonized room partition and a platform on which various types of amphorae were exhibited. They were either locally-made for wine and dried fruit, or imported, such as a Cretan wine amphor. The kitchen is at the back of the room, and a brick bench is clearly visible, nesting large terracotta vases used for food preservation, only partially upset by the Bourbon diggings. The shop is a good example of a business activity going on at the time of the eruption. It is to be remarked that shops occasionally dubbed as the living quarters of their owners, who as a rule resided in the upper-level storage area.

In front of this, at no.10 of *ins.* VI, there is a long service passage from the Thermae which leads to the burner and the heating system (an iron shovel used to feed the furnace is still there) and, up a small ladder, to a large well and its water-lifting system consisting of a bronze water-wheel, which has been already described. Another ladder, placed next to the entry, whose lower wooden part is mostly still preserved, led up to the upper terraces of the Thermae.

Along the sidewalk on the right, at no.7, *ins.* V, next to the food shop, there is the entrance to the small but nicely decorated **House of Neptune and Amphytrites.** The main walls are all in reticulate work. The upper level, supported by beams, conspicuously overhangs the street pavement. The collapse of the external wall allows a glance at the inner arrangement and wall decorations from the outside. On the left of the

Triclinium and nymphaeum of the House of Neptune and Amphytrites

long entrance vestibule there is a small room and a kitchen with the attendant latrine. Then comes a large atrium, now roofless but whose height can be appreciated from the rows of beam holes, with a marble basin in the centre, flanked by the opening of the cistern. The flooring is in terracotta fragments, decorated with polychromic marble flakes. The house was furnished with running water, a feature indicated by clearly exposed lead pipes. In the corner of the atrium there is a nice brick lararium covered with marble slabs, where two of the famous monochromes on Herculaneum marble were discovered. One of these is signed by the Athenian Alexander (as the famous monochrome representing the astragal players, also from Herculaneum), now kept in the National Archaeological Museum in Naples. At the back of the atrium there is a small but elegant tablinum, paved with valuable marble pieces; the walls are decorated with architectural paintings. A central drawing, only partially preserved and almost faded, depicts Narcissus next to a spring. Nearby there is a cubicle paved with white mosaic sporting a black band. Other cubicles abut the atrium.

Frontally from the entrance door and on view through the large tablinum window, the visitor can see, in the summer triclinium, the wall mosaic in glass chips, framed with shells and scoriaceous lava, representing Neptune and Amphytrites in a richly decorated aedicula. However, the correlation between the cult of Neptune and that of Venus

Triclinium and nymphaeum of the House of Neptune and Amphytrites

in the sacred area of the Herculaneum seashore, leads one to think that we are rather dealing with a representation of Venus.

Both deities, in fact, used to protect sailors. On the mosaic side there are some garden frescoes with fountains, conveying the impression of greenery, which did not really exist due to the limited area available. The other side of the summer triclinium is occupied by a nymphaeum with lateral rectangular niches and a larger central arched one, also lined with glass mosaic, shells and scoriaceous lava pieces. The nimphaeum is adorned by elegant vegetal friezes including one with gryphons facing a crater, garlands surmounted by peacocks (Juno's symbols), and deer being chased by dogs. Three marble theatre masks with acroterium functions (a fourth one, found out of place, was put back on its original upper wall) used to remind the clients that life is a comedy, as Augustus said before his death. The room was also decorated with elegant little marble columns.

Still beside the summertime triclinium there is a large vaulted hall paved in mosaic and with rich architectural wall decoration on a white background (the central drawings are missing, having been taken away during the Bourbon age).

Once out of the house and continuing along the right sidewalk, at no.8, *ins.* V, the visitor can enter the wonderful **Pretty Courtyard House**. The doorway opens directly on to a rectangular vestibule paved in white mosaic with a black border. In front there is a small tablinum, its base lower than the courtyard's. Here the flooring is in white mosaic with black cruciform motifs, framed in an elegant ivy band, while the walls are yellow. All around the vestibule there are other small rooms and a corridor leading to a kitchen. The little courtyard is, from an architectural viewpoint, the most beautiful and also the most interesting part of the house, with a masonry stairway on one side, having a nicely shaped parapet. The design of the starway is made lighter by the arched niche upon which it rests, whose inside is elegantly painted with oleanders and ivy garlands on a yellow background. The mouth of the well opens at the bottom of the niche. The courtyard flooring is in white mosaic with thin black swastika motifs positioned in squares. It appears that the fresco on a violet background on the stairway was just about to be finished in 79 A.D.: the eagle contours had been scraped on the bottom of the aedicula while the drawing on the right had just been outlined. On the left of the courtyard, a tastefully frescoed room opens through a large window. This room stands on a slightly lower level, and a corridor from the entrance vestibule leads to it. On the right of the courtyard a large hall is also illuminated through a square window in the south wall, once communicating through a door, later walled in, with the nearby Bicentenary House. The flooring of the hall is in white mosaic framed in a black plaited band. The walls are divided into large yellow squares changing into red as a result of having been exposed to high temperature at the time of the eruption. On the wall at the back of the room there are two beautiful Neoattic marble reliefs of Dawn and Sunset, unearthed in many pieces that were dragged and scattered along the 5th *cardo* by a pyroclastic flow.

Out of the Pretty Courtyard House, after crossing the 4th *cardo* arcade, and continuing on to the secondary entrance and the perimetral wall of the Black Hall House, the visitor attains the *decumanus maximus*. On the left there is a small altar, flanked by two painted snakes, the venue of typical cross-cultural rites (*compitalia*). At the opposite side of the *cardo*, on the protruding mezzanine paved with terracotta fragments and connected with the corner shop, a large quantity of wheat grains were discovered. The small pillar interrupting the road is another *castellum aquae*, regulating water pressure and distribution in the city. On the side towards the *decumanus maximus* the recess once hosting the lead water-ducts is visible and a series of derivations is preserved on the sidewalk. On the pillar, inside a square, there is an interesting edict, painted in black letters, that had been renewed twice. It was firstly promulgated by the *duoviri*, the supreme town officials, and then by the *aediles*, and contains the injunction not to dump rubbish in that area, under penalty of a silver coin for freed men and spanking for slaves.

On the decuman there is a pretty public fountain with a rectangular basin made of solid white limestone slabs; the headpieces are decorated on one side with a Hellenistic picture of a naked Venus wringing out her hair, on the other with a Medusa head.

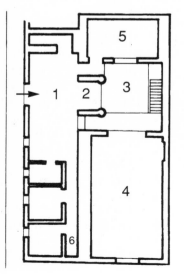

Plan of the Pretty Courtyard House
1 Atrium
2 Tablinum
3 Courtyard
4 Hall
5 Triclinium
6 Latrine

Cubicle of the Tuscan Colonnade House turned into a shop

Triclinium of the Tuscan Colonnade House

Fresco on the end wall of the Tuscan Colonnade House triclinium

Fresco representing Dirce's torture in the House of the Mosaic Atrium

X

**Fresco of Venus and Mars in the
Bicentenary House tablinum**

**Fresco of the Tuscan Colonnade House
triclinium**

View of the decumanus maximus with Hercules fountain

View of the decumanus maximus

Gemstone House and Telephus Relief House

**Atrium of Telephus
Relief House**

Garden of the House of the Stags

Mosaic of Cupids riding hippocampi in the House of the Stags

Seaside view of the House of the Mosaic Atrium and of the House of the Stags, with the imposing Vesuvius profile the far background

Equestrian statue of M. Nonius Balbus.

Bronze dancer

Detail of a warrior's small bronze statue

Bronze statue of Isis-Fortune

Bronze statue of Mercury

Gold coins found beside the fugitives

XVI

THE *DECUMANUS MAXIMUS*

The *decumanus maximus* is the main road, simply paved with pressed earth, so far explored in Herculaneum. Its width is 12.30 metres, and is flanked by comfortable sidewalks. The presence of stone obstacles indicates that carts were not allowed to go through. Due to a great number of shops, this had to be the market place, as witnessed also by a number of charred masts, once carrying sun awnings, still inserted in the middle of the road at excavation time, and the many related holes found on the streetside walls. The 5th *cardo*, which proceeded northwards, and turned at a right angle to the east into the area not yet excavated, coped with vehicular traffic. From the excavations we are also aware of the existence of a public waterwell and of a wheat silo on the northern margin of the road. The road, traced out at the time of the city foundation, proceeded originally eastward, beyond the 5th *cardo*, below the upper hall of the gymnasium complex, built during the Augustan age. The hall, preceded by a pronaos with two columns, closed the perspective of the decuman on that side. On the western side, a large four-faced brick arch built in 49 A.D., once decorated with a rich marble covering, marked the entrance to the arcaded square erroneously called basilica and to the public area of the city. The arch intrados is decorated with caissons and stucco figures (a recumbent Satyr can be admired). Turning to the left, at no.12 (*ins.* VI) there is a shop with a long bench made of second-hand white limestone blocks. The shop, a forger's workshop (*plumbarius*) contains a crucible and some terracotta water vessels, used for cooling metal tools and handicrafts.

In this place lead ingots, pipe sections, two lovely bronze candle-

Reconstructed view of the **decumanus maximus,** *as seen from the east end*

sticks and a little statue of Bacchus inlaid with gold, silver and copper (currently under repair) were found. The upper wooden mezzanine is partly preserved, with some timber still resting on top of it.

At no.13 there is the entrance to the **Black Hall House**, owned by the Augustalis *L. Venidius Ennychus,* whose wax-tablet archives were found in a wooden case on the upper floor.

His eligibility to the title of Augustalis had been questioned, and the

The forger's workshop (plumbarius) *on the* decumanus maximus.

legal proceedings for the validation process are preserved. His name is, in fact, registered on the marble tablets believed to list the Augustales' College members. Terracotta fragments with lines of white mosaic chips pave the spacious atrium, where a tuff basin acts as an impluvium. At its sides there are some cubicles and the kitchen, while at one end there is a large tablinum with fresco remains on a black background. From here it is possible to go forward to a colonnaded peristyle, whose black mosaic flooring is decorated with polychromic marble flakes. At the far end, located at one side of the back-entrance from the 4th *cardo,* there are two low-vaulted rooms with an exceptionally well-preserved painted ceiling; the second room is also lit from a small courtyard at the back, which has a masonry lararium. On the opposite side there is a huge hall, floored in white mosaic, with various wall and ceiling drawings painted on a black background, whence the name of the house was derived. A marble table and a nice wooden lararium were found in this hall. To the side of this, preceded by a vestibule, the visitor can see a mosaic-paved cubicle, with beautiful wall drawings and the remains of landscape sketches painted on a red background.

Returning to the entrance, on the left (at no.14), an attractive **shop**

Bacchus statuette found in the forger's workshop on the *decumanus maximus,* after its restoration

Peristyle of P. Venidius Ennychus House or Black Hall House.

sign-board can be admired. On the upper part there is a divinity figure, *Semo Sancus* — often identified with Hercules — whom it was customary to swear on in business transactions, with the inscription: *ad Sancum*.

On the lower part of the sign-board there is a bright rectangular panel with four pitchers, indicated as *cucumae* (*ad cucumas*: the word still survives in some Italian dialects such as, for instance, Apulian, with the meaning of "vase") showing prices per *sextarius* (about half a litre) of wine according to the quality. The lower panel with the inscription NOLA in big red letters is a stage-show announcement, found beneath the now re-positioned upper panel at the time when the latter was detached from the wall in order to consolidate it. In small black letters, between the L and the A, it is possible to read the the author's signature, *scr*[iptor] *Aprilis a Capua,* something of special significance because it shows that such artists could be itinerant. Going on the visitor will find a shop with an upper wooden platform and a mezzanine that can be reached up a stairway (at no.15; notice the charred falling beam), and another shop connected with the atrium of the Tuscan Colonnade House; in fact this shop was originally an elegant cubicle of the house (no.16), paved with valuable marble (removed during the Bourbon age) and rendered more attractive with frescoes on a red and light-blue background, which are well preserved on one side. These include a nice frieze depicting Hercules and the sacrifice of a bull, not unlike of the consecration of the *Ara Maxima* in the *Forum Boarium* in Rome, and some caryatides on the upper part. Noteworthy are also the perfectly preserved wooden shelves protruding on to the sidewalk.

The **Tuscan Colonnade House** (*ins.* VI, no.17), probably belonging to a certain *L. Marius*, according to a seal on a lead pipe found nearby, was rebuilt during the Augustan age, just before the construction of the Augustales' College on an older republican layout. The old atrium nucleus, exhibiting two stages of terracotta fragment flooring, and featuring a marble impluvium, shows, on the right side, a hall with mosaic carpet on the threshold framed by a Greek fret — the hall itself being paved in white mosaic contoured by a double black band. On the III style decoration of the walls two drawings are still visible, the one on the left portraying two sitting mythical figures, the other, on the back wall, depicting a conversation between two women. The frieze shows elegant formal architectural motives: on the back wall a niche was walled in,

Wooden lararium, with marble capitals, from the Black Saloon House

whereupon a frescoed picture was done on the spot in order to complete the decoration. In front of the entrance there is a large tablinum which reflects the Vitruvian canons; the threshold is decorated with a meandering band including other small motifs (chess-board, etc.) and the flooring consists of white mosaic framed in black bands. The IV style wall decoration, redone after the earthquake of 62 A.D., presents a two-colour baseboard (black and violet-brown), and the central part of the walls with red and light-blue panels separated by wide vertical bands decorated with rich garlands, among which some Ocean masks can be seen. The lateral panels only have some small circles in the centre. The upper frieze is very rich and shows a complex system of formal buildings surmounted by big acroteria.

Through a corridor, on the left of which there is a large tuff-block stairway leading to the upper level surmounted by a mezzanine where a deposit of amphorae was found, the visitor can reach a large peristyle surrounded by brick columns which were originally fluted and then smoothed and painted white in the upper part and alternatingly in red and black in the lower part. On the top there were some terracotta antefixes with a Gorgon mask, now removed. On the left there is a cubicle paved in white mosaic framed by a double black band and, on the threshold, elegant black and white triangular motifs. On the right there is a large triclinium paved in white, black and yellow mosaic and a central inset with geometric motifs of commuting octagons and triangles. The wall decoration in the back side is well preserved; it presents formal architectural motifs in the frieze, with caryatids on the sides and a citharist Apollo in the centre, a peacock strolling in the direction of a fruit basket, and a sherped's crook in the lunette. In the nearby side, where the secondary entrance corridor on the 3rd *cardo* opens, lies the service quarter comprised of a kitchen and a small altar with a stereotype drawing of two snakes. On the peristyle three other cubicles, elegantly decorated in the IV style, with beautiful white and black mosaic flooring, open up, one still preserving a III-style ceiling. An upper storey extended over the entire house, part of which was also reachable independently, up a stairway, from the 3rd *cardo*. In one of the rooms fourteen golden coins and a bronze seal of a certain *M. Co* (-). *Fru* (-) were found.

Out of the Tuscan Colonnade House, and going back along the *decumanus maximus*, the visitor can admire on the opposite side of the road a brick portico (only the façade is still standing) with recessed shops, two of which were partially explored. In one of them there was a variety of foodstuff (corn, millet, dates, broad beans, chick-peas, olives, figs, oak galls, lentils, walnuts, carobs, pine seeds, onions), while in the other a box of glass vases still packed in straw, from a factory in Pozzuoli owned by a *P. Gessius Ampliatus,* was discovered. The corner pillar with the northward extension of the 4th *cardo* (the last one on the right before the three-storey building) hosts an unmistakable phallic symbol believed to keep the evil eye away. Continuing past the fountain of Venus, on the right there is a foodshop with a nice marble bench and large terracotta containers (*dolii*). At no.11 (*ins.* V) there is a small atrium house with a marble puteal, perhaps originally annexed to the nearby Bicentenary House. The tablinum is very elegant and has a very rich marble flooring contoured by a black and white mosaic band with greenery turnings and central little palm-trees. A black and white meandering mosaic band adorns the threshold. The walls present IV-style frescoes with two central drawings of a seated citharist Apollo, a woman standing by his side and a young boy drawn on an architectural background, plus Selene and Endymion. Three buried *dolii* along the atrium wall show that the house underwent a business-type transformation in the latter part of the city life. In the shop at no.12, a high wooden shelf is still preserved, on which remnants of sorghum brooms were piled up, and are now on view.

At no.15 there is the entrance to the **Bicentenary House**, probably owned by one of the important local families,

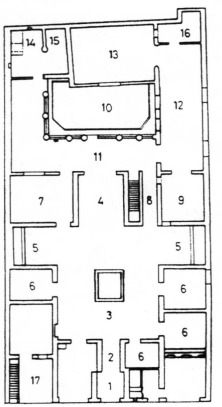

1 Fauces (entrance corridor)
2 Vestibule
3 Atrium
4 Tablinum
5 Alae
6 Cubicles
7 Triclinium
8 Corridor
9 Oecus (hall)
10 Viridarium (garden)
11 Porch
12 Windowed porch
13 Oecus (hall)
14 Kitchen
15 Latrine
16 Cella penaria (food store)
17 Shop

Bicentenery House plan

71

the *Calatorii*, according to what is shown on the of wax-tablets archive of *Calatoria Themis*, widow of a certain *C. Petronius Stephanus*. The archive included the documents related to the impassionate and moving court proceedings in the case of Justa, a little girl whose free-state at birth was doubted, and was therefore contended by two women. The house was dug out in 1938, the second centenary from the beginning of Herculaneum excavations, and therefore it was given the name it now holds.

The house has a traditional type of plan and dates back to the

View of the Bicentenary House atrium

Augustan age. The vestibule and atrium are paved in black mosaic with bands and geometrical motifs made of white chips. A plaited mosaic frame encloses the central marble basin of the atrium, whose walls present a very simple IV-style decoration with a black baseboard, dark red background and a vivid red frieze. Above the stucco frame the plaster was left white. The rooms which open around the atrium have thresholds outlined by mosaic panels or marble bands. The right side area, a rectangular sitting room, entirely open on to the atrium, shows a seared reticulate wooden gate, with an elaborate frame, mostly still preserved. Notice the brick podium which supported some wooden wardrobes. The tablinum is elegantly decorated with a marble threshold and a black mosaic band on a white background with stylized leaf motives. The floor is made of white mosaic with black bands and a central rectangular area of choice marble pieces forming a polychromic carpet framed by a plaited motif. The wall decoration shows a black baseboard with shrubs; a background characterised by red squares separated by greenery bands, with central drawings and medallions (coupled busts of Satyrs and Bacchantes); frame contours on a black background with scenes of hunting Cupids, a frieze with formal architectural views and stucco frame. The central painting on the right depicts Pasiphae showing Daedalus a heifer to be taken by the artist as a model (Pasiphae, Minos' wife, in love with an incredibly beautiful bull, in order to be mounted by the beast, devised the trick of entering a heifer sculpture, made by Daedalus. From this union the Minotaur was born). In the central drawing on the left Venus and Mars are shown along with three Cupids. On the left of the tablinum there is a triclinium with flooring in white mosaic, communicating both with the atrium and the arcaded garden, at the end of which the kitchen and the latrine are located. The garden, where roses were grown, is flanked on two sides only by a porch with fluted and stuccoed columns. Behind the garden is a large hall paved with terracotta shards. In an apartment on the upper floor a rectangular stucco panel with a cross imprint can be seen on the wall, indicating the previous presence of some wooden structure. When this was discovered it sparked a famous discussion on the possibility of a Christian meaning. The recent discovery of cruciform wooden shelves at Villa Regina in Boscoreale put to rest the Christian connection.

In one of the upper floor apartments, on the western side of the atrium, a bronze seal of a certain *M. Helvius Eros* was found.

Once out of the Bicentenary House, at no.17 there is a shop with the back-room decorated in elegant IV-style frescoes. The family quarters are on the upper level, which can be reached via an internal wooden stairway next to the entrance. On the left of the shop entrance there is a terracotta dolium and close by a small hearth and a cabinet with three wooden shelves. The visitor will also notice a terracotta stove. In the upper storey, inserted in a wall, an attractive fresco drawing in a wooden frame was found and promptly recovered. The drawing depicts some Cupids around a tripod. Also from the first floor of the house came a wooden wardrobe and a lararium, now on view near the entrance.

In front of the shop, on the opposite side of the *Decumanus Maximus* a structure consisting of at least three storeys was found, probably dating from the post-Claudian age, which was built in a "high-rise" fashion to best exploit the limited space available within the city walls at that time. Only its front side has been excavated, showing an arcade with rectangular brick pillars and semi-columns, and a mezzanine accessible up a wooden stairway that proved impossible to preserve. Instead the remains of two wooden doors belonging to the shops in the back, and the shutters of a first floor window, are preserved. On the last pillar on the right there is an inscription in red letters which has almost faded out, being the only Herculaneum electoral manifesto discovered. The local competition for office was evidently quite soft-toned, contrary to what was evidenced by over 2,000 Pompeii electoral graffiti. The inscription refers to a candidate quaestor, *M. Caecilius Potitus*. At this point the visitor has reached the corner with the 5th *cardo*, where an attractive public fountain, decorated with a mask of Hercules, can be seen. The corner shop (*ins.* V, no.21) has a sales-counter with *dolii* severely damaged by the Bourbon excavators, and a latrine.

In front there is a large rectangular hall which closed the path of the *Decumanus Maximus*. The hall was preceded by a pronaos with two tuff columns and was subdivided by two other travertine columns. The flooring is in black mosaic with polychromic marble flakes and white bands, while the walls were decorated in the IV style. On the right, a corridor leads to a long loggia with mosaics, part of the palaestra, flanked by a number of rooms nicely decorated with mosaics, while in a central one where fine marble was employed instead. From the loggia it was possible to enjoy the show offered by the athletic games taking place in the lower terrace. The palaestra was built at the same time as the previously mentioned rectangular hall, i.e., during the Augustan age. Excavations proved that both were built on the extension of the *decumanus maximus*. It is probably right to identify this place, connected with the Herculaneum campus, with the centre of the local *Iuventus*, that is the college where the city youth assembled.

THE FIFTH UPPER *CARDO* AND THE PALAESTRA
THE LOWER DECUMAN

Turning left, the visitor starts going down to the 5th *cardo*, a bit wider than the others and paved anew with white limestone to grant it a superior monumental appearance. On the left, in fact, is the huge Palaestra complex, built in reticulate work, an Augustan period addition to the regular urban plan, but at an angle with it. The complex was the campus of the ancient city, and included the arcaded esplanade used for gymnastic exercises and sport activities, with a promenade sided by trees, and places used for cults. Due consideration was given to maintenance costs for this public building: in the front side a series of small houses and shops with an upper level were built which, rented or sold, provided money for the running costs. Among these a dye-works is at no.17-18, and at no.13 a shop with a brick bench and terracotta *dolii* containing corn, broad beans and chick-peas. The shop was owned, as recorded on a bronze seal unearthed on the spot, by a certain *A. Fuferius*. At no. 11 there is another dye-works, and at no.10 the remains of an inlaid small loom, a stool and a wooden bed were put in the back room. In the latter there was the skeleton of an adolescent. A certain number of gems in a wooden case were also found: some cut and engraved, others still rough.

View of the 5th upper *cardo* with the Palaestra vestibule

Workshop-house (*ins. orientalis* 1, n.10), with its furnishings

Some lapidary tools, a miniature altar with a dedication to Hercules and a beautiful marble portrait, believed to be of M. Nonius Balbus, were also found in the case. It is conjectured that the owner of this comfortable workshop-house must have been a freedman of the above said remarkable personage. At no.9 there was a place where wine was sold: still preserved is a platform, a ladder and an attractive lararium in a plastered niche with frescoed pictures of Hercules, Mercury and Bacchus; below, two snakes face each other on a garden background. In the back shop there are the remains of a charred wooden bed.

At no.8 the visitor can enter the **bakery** which it is known to have been owned by a certain *Sex. Patulcius Felix,* his bronze seal having been found in the mezzanine. Note also two "piperno" mill grindstones which were worked by donkeys, kept in a stable in the back. On the left the visitor can see a large oven with a phallic symbol above the opening. Another similar symbol was hanging from the wall. A whole series of bronze baking-pans was recovered during the excavations. The shop at no.6 shows a well-preserved bench with four terracotta *dolii.* The workshop at no.5, just before the Palaestra entrance, was probably a dyer's shop, due to the presence of a furnace made from a large *dolium* which was perforated and walled up.

On the right, still going down the 5th upper *cardo*, at no.22 (*ins.* V) there is a stairway leading to an upper-level apartment where, in a wood-

The oven of the bakery owned by Sex. *Patulcius Felix*

en case, the rich archives of *L. Cominius Primus* were discovered, and, in another case, the bronze seal of a certain *Q. Iunius Philadespotes*. A well preserved wooden bed was also discovered in this apartment. At no.24, between two shops, there is the entrance to a small house, with a lararium niche and two snakes painted in the atrium.

At no.30 there is the entrance to the **Corinthian Atrium House** which preserves the original dimensions of the Oscan urban layout. Going up three steps and through the vestibule the visitor can enter the colonnaded atrium with three brick columns on each side (whence the name of the house), paved with fragments of pottery decorated with polychromic marble slabs. Between the columns is a low pluteus delimiting the central impluvium, with platbands where in the middle is a small cruciform marble basin (at the intersection of the arms there are traces of a fountain). The room on the right side of the entrance shows an attractive mosaic flooring with geometrical drawings in a recurring stylized motif of a sacred two-edged axe, with a central purple marble square plate framed in a leafy band and crenellated towers. On the opposite side is the kitchen with a latrine and a brick stairway leading to the upper storey. In front is the large tablinum with red and yellow base-band and black background alternating with dark red pillars. Laterally there are two cubicles, one of which shows some little drawings of naval battles. On the left there is another elegantly decorated room, whose ceiling still preserves its vaulted and intricately lacunar design.

Following on, at no.31 (*ins.* V), is the **Wooden Sacellum House**, with a tuff-block doorway. The plan is very simple, the construction in rubble masonry. In a corridor there are some decorations in the 1st Pompeiian style. The atrium has the impluvium basin made of tuff and a terracotta puteal above the mouth of the underlying cistern. On the entrance side there is a cubicle where a charred wooden lararium cabinet was found, hence the name given to the house. The tablinum is positioned at the far side of the house. Through a corridor two other rooms and the kitchen can be reached. On the upper level, in a case under a charred bed, an archive of waxed tablets was found and, together with it, an interesting limestone matrix, bearing the initials L. T., used to make six lead tablets, among which is a caduceus and, on the opposite side, the *Tithasus* surname (probably corresponding to that of a man mentioned in the so-called College roster of the Augustales, whose family connections are unfortunately lost). On the ground floor the lararium cabinet, after which the house is named, was found containing the bronze seal of a certain *L. Autronius Euthymus*.

The entrance to the Large Doorway House

Once at the intersection between the 5th *cardo* and the lower decuman, turning right at no.35 (*ins.* V), one finds the entrance to the **Large Doorway House**, immediately after a shop once connected to the same house. It is so called from the nice doorway with semicolumns and ornamented platband built after the earthquake of 62 A.D. The semicolums have Hellenistic capitals cut from a tufaceous rock decorated with orch-bearing Victories. The house was originally part of the Samnitic House. In the walls of the entrance vestibule there are included two grooved shafts of tuff columns and two pillars with semicolumns, still in their original position. Replacing the atrium there is a long transverse room lit by a small courtyard, which was used as an impluvium for collecting water in the cistern below. A vast triclinium is right in front of the entrance, flanked on the right by two cubicles. The decoration of the far-end walls is still partly preserved: it consists of a central drawing representing the old Silenus sitting with two Satyrs and watching Bacchus and Ariadne at the feet of a column with a divinity. The next exedra has a nice frieze with curtains opening on garden views with birds and little Cupids intent on picking flowers. A corridor leads to the kitchen and the latrine, and to the ladder the tenants used to get to the upper level. On the back wall of the vestibule there is a drawing with two birds pecking at a butterfly and some cherries. Finally the visitor can reach a small room on the side of the courtyard, with IV-style frescoes on a light blue monochrome background. Here slender architectural artwork is enhanced by tritons, centaurs and gryphons acting as acroters, tripods, drapery, a frieze with a trophy in the middle, arms hung from the ceiling and theatre masks.

Out of the Large Doorway House the visitor can return to the intersection between the lower decuman and the 5th *cardo*. In front of this, two steps higher, is the monumental pronaos with two tuff columns, one of the entrances to the **Palaestra**, the vast Augustan-age complex. Actually, this is the Herculaneum campus, the porticoed area used as a venue for exercises, athletics and sport games (including a swimming pool). The area was also used for walks, teaching (under the arcade) and worship. The large gymnasium vestibule was mistakenly identified in Bourbon times as the *Mater Deum* temple due to an inscription found on the pronaos with the date 76 A.D., celebrating the restoration of this temple, financed by the Emperor Vespasian, after the damage inflicted by the devastating earthquake of 62 A.D. However, the inscription was deposited here only temporarily, as in the gymnasium there were some works in progress, based on some roofing slabs imprited with a bull and a lion facing each other (also connected with the cult to Cybele), stored on the mosaic flooring of a room accessible from the far end of the cryptoporticus: evidently the temple was somewhere nearby, in an area not yet excavated. On the higher area of the Palaestra there was probably a temple dedicated to Egyptian deities, as indicated by a basalt statue of the god Atoun, an original sculpture of the Ptolemaic times, fallen beside the rectangular basin, and by an interesting small bronze base with pseudo-hieroglyphs unearthed in a position which indicates it was dragged by a pyroclastic flow along the 5th *cardo*, up to the Palaestra entrance.

The vestibule, with a rectangular base-plan, had a vaulted ceiling decorated with a myriad of alternating red, green and yellow stars. From here the western porch of the gymnasium can be accessed, of which it was possible to reconstruct the sculptural decoration: in the southwest corner a beautiful copy of the so-called "Gardens' Aphrodites" was erected, following a dream, by a certain *Iulia Hygia*. In the opposite corner, on a masonry base, was a copy of the "Fréjus Aphrodites", while in the northwestern corner beckoned a statue of Augustan age, a portrait characterised by heroic nudity.

The lower terrace of the Palaestra is made up of a large rectangular (about 60 x 78 m) area once shaded by trees, porticoed on three sides, while the fourth, the northern side, is occupied by a cryptoporticus with windows, marked by semicolumns with a number of appendages (in one of them note the signatures of travellers, dated 1749 to 1753) and a stairway leading to the vaulted upper level.

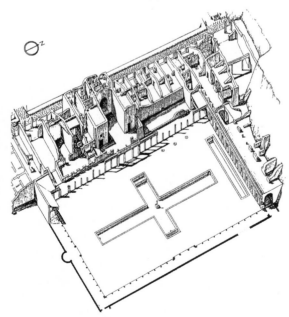

Elevation of the Palaestra (after Maiuri, 1958)

Egyptian black limestone statue of the god Atoun, found in the Palaestra (Ptolemaic age)

The cryptoporticus supports the upper terrace already described. At the centre of the western side, emphasised by a Corinthian-type prominence of the portico, there is the opening of a vast rectangular apse-ended room, almost ten metres high, flanked by two smaller vaulted rooms and preceded by a vestibule.

The place is paved with little pieces of rare marble and is richly dec-

View of the Palaestra western side

orated with IV-style architectural motifs, partly removed during the 17th century and now in the National Archaeological Museum in Naples.

The back of the room has a large niche with a marble desk in front, used for the award ceremony of prizes in the athletic and sports games, as well as for the Emperor's worship. In the lateral halls two headless togaed marble statues are displayed: they come from the suburban temple of Venus in the Sacred Area. The halls, paved in mosaic and painted white, present one of the best III-style fresco specimens, with elements inspired by Egyptian iconography.

The floor of the next long rectangular room on the left was raised after the earthquake in 62 A.D. on a landfill of earth and fragments of pottery. On that occasion the brick base, with fresco remains next to the wall, was buried. On the wall near the cryptoporticus entrance a small fresco can be seen of Hercules as a child, in the act of strangling some snakes.

A long, deep, rectangular basin flanking the cryptoporticus, lined with pottery fragments and with side-holes, made of discarded amphora necks, providing the fish shelter from sun rays, was successively filled with earth and replaced by a much larger central cruciform pool. At the

The bronze fountain of the Palaestra with Lerna's Hydra

intersection of the arms, on a masonry base, rises the cast of a large bronze fountain of the Hydra Lernaea, a five-headed snake monster killed by Hercules, the hero linked to the name and legend of the origins of the city. The visitor can observe the Bourbon tunnels which may help to figure out the plan of the two sides still unexcavated. A large drain pipe allowed the pool to be emptied into a big vaulted underground conduit built along the eastern sidewalk of the 5th *cardo*.

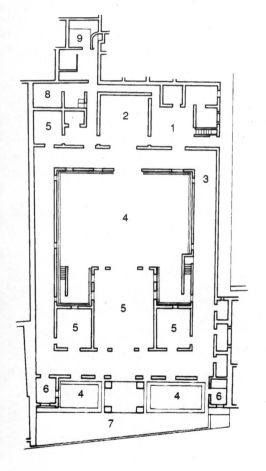

**Plan of the House
of the Stags**
1 Atrium
2 Triclinium
3 Cryptoporticus
4 Garden with sculptures
5 Hall
6 Daytime cubicles
7 Lodge
8 Alcove
9 Kitchen

THE FIFTH LOWER *CARDO*

Once out of the Palaestra the visitor can admire, at the intersection, the public fountain decorated with Neptune's head between two dolphins. Immediately to the right, at the corner (*ins.* IV, no.16), there is a tavern with a marble-covered bench, terracotta *dolii* and marble-clad staggered shelves used to store vases for drinks and food. On the room partition immediately behind there is a coarse painting of a ship and some graffiti, the most interesting of which, in Greek, is a "politically-incorrect" saying of the cynic philosopher Diogenes (the one who lived in a barrel): "Diogenes, the Cynic, seeing a woman swept away by a flood, said: Let a calamity sweep away another calamity". The tavern is connected to a small atrium house, with two rooms containing IV-style frescoes still partly preserved. The one nearer the street was roughly divided in two by a partition in the last phase preceding the eruption.

At no.17 there is another tavern with a sales counter and an half-buried closet, lined with potsherds, used for storing victuals. On the right there is a partly buried *dolium* marked with a number: it contained some walnuts. On the facing wall is a fresco representing the owner of the tavern himself, near the *dolium*, and a big Priapus, whose task was to keep away the evil-eye from the premises.

The corner of the lower decuman with the 5th *cardo*, and Neptune's Fountain

84

In the backshop there is a brick seat. Even in this instance the tavern was connected to a small house with a tetrastyle atrium and an upper level.

At no.19-20 is the small **Cloth House**, so called after some linen sheets discovered in it, with a wooden stairway to the upper level. At no. 21 is the entrance to the **House of the Stags**, which is flanked by a brick seat. Because of the discovery of a piece of carbonised bread with a seal, it is known that the house was owned by *Q. Granius Verus,* one of the city elders. The house is the best example of the transformation which took place in the traditional atrium house, leading to more monumental solutions — influenced by the architecture of the large seaside villas — built, as it were, in a position which aimed at providing a better view of the superb seascape of the gulf of Naples. The tiny, covered atrium, is furnished with a gallery and a service quarter on the upper level. From the atrium a long corridor on the right leads directly to the kitchen, while on the left the visitor can enter a large windowed cryptoporticus, paved in white mosaic decorated with a black band and polychrome marble flakes. The walls show an elegant frescoed decoration, with drawings of Cupids playing with the weapons of Mars and Hercules (club and bow), or occupied in various activities, as well as still-life and seascape drawings. Some of these painted panels, removed during the Bourbon period (the western wall is cut by a tunnel), can be seen in the National Archaeological Museum in Naples. The cryptoporticus includes a garden where two round marble tables were found, together with a vase and some sculptures; their castings have been now placed in their original position. They represent two deer attacked by dogs, a drunken Hercules, and a Satyr holding a goatskin-fountain. On one side of the garden there is a nice marble puteal.

Following the garden axis northwards one reaches a large hall, enhanced by a tympanum of blue glassy pulp with a frieze depicting Cupids riding sea-animals and a big central head of Oceanus. The hall is paved with quality marble and has walls frescoed in the IV style on a black background. On one side there is a smaller marble-floored hall with wall decorations on a red background, and a well-preserved ceiling (with Minerva's helmeted head in the middle). A bronze bath tub in good shape, which was found in a corridor connected to the garden, is situated here. From this smaller hall, through a corridor, the visitor can get to the well-preserved kitchen. On the side there is an alcove, also paved in marble, containing a pretty IV-style decoration on a red background.

On the sea side of the House of the Stags there is another large hall with fragments of a high-quality marble pavement, and windows opening on to the garden. Note the remains of frescoed decorations with a

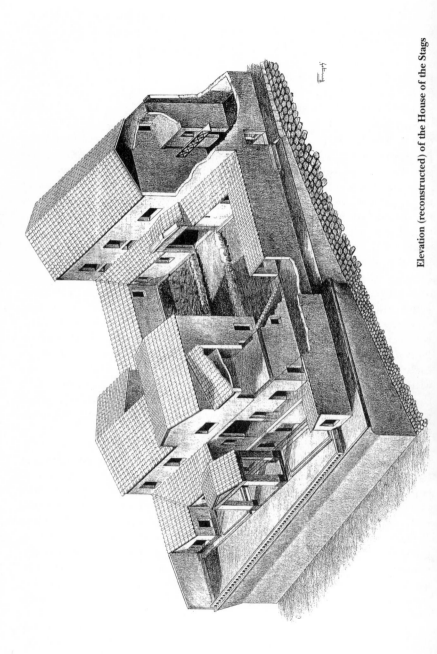

Elevation (reconstructed) of the House of the Stags

Seaside view of the House of the Stags

picture of a suppliant Cassandra on a yellow background. Two rooms on the sides of the hall are also paved with choice marble (note the threshold of the room to the west, consisting of a large oriental alabaster slab) and an elegant frescoed decoration.

Facing the sea there is an open gallery and an arbour resting on four pillars: underneath, one of the marble tables found in the garden has been placed.

Once out of the House of the Stags and crossing to the opposite sidewalk, there is the entrance (at no.2) to **Telephus' Relief House**, one of the largest and most finely decorated Herculaneum houses. Due to its connection with the Suburban Thermae it is reasonable to include this Augustan-age house among the likely possessions of the senator M. Nonius Balbus. The atrium is particularly sumptuous, presenting, on three sides, stuccoed columns painted in red. The wall decoration is also on a red background. The central marble basin is graced by a flower pot. Between the columns hang the casts of marble *oscilla* (small masks) found here, while the cast of the Neoattic marble relief with two scenes of Telephus' myth (Telephus was the illegitimate son of Hercules) hangs from a wall. The originals are currently kept in the National Archaeological Museum in Naples. On the left there is Achilles consulting an oracle, who reveals to him that in order to conquer Troy, he will have to cure the wound of a hero — Telephus — which he himself had inflicted. The scene with the healing of the wound is at the side. At the end of the atrium the visitor can see the mosaic-paved tablinum (on its right there is a cubicle paved with terracotta fragments and decorations of white mosaic chips, and a simple, linear wall decoration on a white background). On the side there is a steeply descending corridor, at the left end of which is the kitchen, then the visitor gets to a very big peristyle, with a central rectangular basin. The garden area is paved with clay tiles. On the southern side the garden is flanked by three rooms paved with rare marble pieces and mosaics, and a corridor leading to two other rooms: in one of them the relief of Telephus was found. From this place the visitor can also reach a spectacular sea-facing hall, paved and lined with varicoloured marble, and marble pilaster-strips surmounted by Corinthian capitals. The airy openings allowed the inhabitants to enjoy the beauty of the landscape and the sea breezes, and to access a balcony surrounding the house on three sides.

On the cliff-side the house had two lower levels with a portico and a vaulted ambulatory. In the middle level, underneath the aforesaid hall, there is a room similarly paved with quality marble extending to the base-boards. It also contains a prestigious wall decoration made of superimposed friezes, some with leafy garlands and bird metopes on rich hanging carpets. The lowermost level, straight on the seashore, and only in recent times partly excavated, yielded a triclinium and a lead water-pipe which perhaps supplied a fountain. Both these lower levels can now be reached from the terrace covering the Suburban Thermae and from the ancient seashore.

Once out of Telephus' Relief House, the visitor can go to no.1, the nearby **Gemstone House**. Their owners probably enjoyed some sort of relationship, since the garden windows of the Gemstone House open on to the peristyle of Telephus' Relief House. The Tuscan-style atrium has three pillars on each of the two opposite sides, standing rather close to the walls to support the wooden beams, and two columns in the last span. The central basin, surrounded by a marble frame, has a lead water-pipe that supplied a fountain. The pavement is in black mosaic with variegated marble chips laid down in geometric patterns. On the walls there are remains of IV-style decorations on a black background, with red baseboard. At the centre of the third span, on the left, there is a painting of a naked Bacchus, holding a thyrsus in his left hand. On the right a room, paved with terracotta shards, has red and black squares as wall decoration. At the end of the atrium there is a big room with mosaic flooring and a central carpet of polychrome marble around a red marble disc. The room has a spacious window open on to the garden, which includes a large basin in its centre. On the right, there is the corridor entrance to the rustic quarter with the well-preserved latrine and kitchen. In the latrine, a graffito by emperor Titus' doctor, *Apollinaris*, is clearly visible, indicating that he had taken good advantage of the facility (*Apollinaris medicus Titi Imperatoris hic cacavit bene* — blissfully relieved himself here).

The three levels of Telephus' Relief House

At the opposite corner, through another windowed corridor, which is open on to the garden (on a brick pillar there is a marble sun-dial), the visitor can get to the living and meeting quarters of the house, unfolding on a seaward portico terminating at both ends with two tiny lodges. Worthy of note in this area is an almost square (5.30 x 6.70m) dining-room, paved in white mosaic with black bands and a central large rectangular panel divided into 20 parts, each with various geometric drawings all around a median rosette. On the side there is an alcove preceded by a vestibule. The alcove is paved with pottery shards dotted with marble flakes, and shows a wall decoration imitating marble cladding. On the opposite side there is another alcove also preceded by a vestibule. This one has white mosaic flooring and wall decorations on a yellow and red background.

Once out of the Gemstone House, from the barrel-vaulted passage descending to the Suburban Thermae, down some steps on the left, the visitor can enter a small house, immediately below the Gemstone House, consisting of a long open gallery, later transformed into a win-dowed vestibule-cryptoporticus serving as an entrance hall, as well as some vaulted rooms underneath the Gemstone House. In 1940 there was an important discovery: the skeletons of a group of fugitives in one of the rooms, which are paved with black and white mosaics. The third room on the left, a square exedra with a wide opening on to the cryp-toporticus, has a white mosaic floor, with a central decoration in black framed by a meandering band. A long corridor leads to the kitchen which is located right behind the line of rooms facing the outside. The inscription on a small marble plaque found in the house tells of a cer-tain *Diomedes*, a slave, *magister dispensator* (master dispenser) dedicating something to the Lares and to the *familia*. A rocking cradle with some hardly recognizable traces of a little skeleton was also found, along with a tiny mattress of dried leaves. A wooden case dragged between the alcove and its vestibule (the room at the end of the open gallery), con-tained some gems, three of them engraved. From the most beautiful of the lot, the name for the house described above was wrongly derived. A bronze seal with the name *M. Pilius Primigenius Granianus*, found in the same carbonized wooden case, identifies the last owner.

Going back to the 5th lower *cardo* along the sidewalk on the right, at no.3 the rustic quarter of Telephus' Relief House, with the wheelwright entrance to the stable, can be visited. Beside is a beautiful garden, now a quiet, shaded place to rest, with a small *sacellum* and three rustic rooms. There are moreover some small rooms built during the Augustan period, plastered smooth and paved with potsherds or just beaten earth, belonging to Telephus' Relief House.

Following along in the same direction one gets to a side-street, lead-ing to a bakery with oven, "piperno" (a volcanic rock) grindstones and a well-preserved stable. Through a small opening, roughly cut in a wall, it is possible to enter a medium-sized house, with remnants of elegant wall decorations, partly removed during the Seventeenth century and recently identified among the frescoes kept in the National Archaeological Museum in Naples. The house has a mosaic flooring, and was annexed to the bakery in the latter part of the city life. It can be accessed through a long corridor directly from the 5th *cardo*, at no.2, past the small shop at the corner with the side street (no.1). In the room opening on to the side street, which has a large window and an exedra niche, an interesting example of a "piperno" cylindrical dough mixer can be observed. Inside, around a central iron device, some wooden blades rotated, while side holes, at varying heights, were used to drain excess water from the mixture.

THE THEATRE

Turning left along Corso Resina upon leaving the archaeological park, and proceding beyond Piazza Plebiscito — where a column surmounted by a bronze statuette celebrates the 1861 unufication of Italy — corresponding to no.123 of Via Mare is the entrance to the Theatre, an illustrious monument and the starting point of the Vesuvian excavations (access is for the time being is restricted to archaeologists only, due to works ion progress).

The access rooms were refurbished in 1849 in Pompeiian style by the architect Giuseppe Settembre, and restored, as stated by the inscription on the façade, in 1865. In the lobby, photographs of the various plans of the monument so far drawn are on display. They include the oldest one, that surveyed by Alcubierre between 1738 and 1747, recording with broken lines the tunnels previously excavated by d'Elboeuf in 1710; the only surviving ones of the Weber and La Vega series; those in the splendid 1783 Piranesi volume; the two by Abbé de Saint-Non published at the end of the 18th century; the plans included in the book by M. Ruggiero *Storia degli scavi di Ercolano* issued in 1885; and finally those executed under this writer's directions. Some other photographs show how the visit to the Theatre took place in the 17th-18th century, when

Title-page of F. Piranesi book *Il Teatro di Ercolano*, published in 1783

91

tourists were escorted by a torch-bearing custodian holding a small printed guidebook enabling them to follow pre-set itineraries (such photographs are reproductions of an oil-painting by L. Lemasle illustrating the 1815 visit by King Joachim Murat's sons, now in the Capodimonte Museum in Naples, and of a print by the famous19th-century landscapist Giacinto Gigante). Not much has changed since, except for the installation of an electrical lighting system, and the visit still introduces us to the exciting atmosphere of the 18th-century discoveries. A 1749 engraving shows a festival held in Rome on the occasion of a ceremonial visit to the Pope by the King of Naples Ferdinand II of Bourbon, the scene being inspired by the Herculaneum Theatre. Also, there are the portraits of a number of the main characters involved in the 18th-century excavations.

In the centre of the room stands a maquette, made of wood and cork and once coloured, executed in 1808 by Domenico Padiglione for teaching purposes.

In 1710-1711, in the course of the first diggings by d'Elboeuf, many of the statues adorning the scene were discovered and removed: among them the already mentioned "Three Herculaneum Ladies", forwarded to Vienna as a gift to Eugene of Savoy and now in the Dresden Museum; their photographs are also in the lobby, along with an attempted reconstruction of the marble cladding of the scene, sadly almost totally taken away at discovery time for undignified re-use elsewhere.

Located at the northwestern edge of the old city, near the Forum, the Herculaneum Theatre was erected in the Augustan age due to the munificence of the *duovir L. Annius Mammianus Rufus,* based on drawings by the architect *P. Numisius,* as declared by an inscription, now in

Maquette of the Herculaneum Theatre, executed in 1808 by D. Padiglione

the National Archaeological Museum in Naples, repeated several times in different places. Its design only partly follows the canons laid down in the contemporary architectural treatise by Vitruvius.

The Theatre is entirely built in masonry while its structural elements are in tufaceous reticulate work, except for the outer pilasters of the walls and the front-side of the stage, which are in brickwork. Its dimensions are 54x41 metres, and it could accommodate up to 2500 spectators, based on an estimate of 50cm of sitting space per person.

Down a first flight of stairs is a small chamber where a number of marble pieces have been collected, the result of the last excavations in the Bourbon era: notably a column's shaft, a Corinthian capital, and fragments of decorated eaves pertaining to the stage. Going left from here, past a long tunnel dug in the tuff, one reaches a small 18th-century balcony opening on a large light shaft cut in 1739, which allows us to see part of the *media cavaea* tiers of seats of the central section. Going back on one's own steps, a sloping passage then leads down to the summit of the *media cavaea*, whose top wall was originally covered with marble slabs and eaves, now revealed by their imprints. On the northern side is a decoration of imitation white-stucco ashlar on a red socle. Higher up is the *summa cavaea* with three steps and three pairs of pedestals for bronze equestrian statues. On the central summit of the *cavaea* there is a small temple and laterally an *aedicula* with marble columns.

An arched doorway leads to a large vaulted corridor running round the outside of the summit of the *media cavaea*, which was used at show-time to regulate the influx of spectators to the tiered seats: it was accessible directly from the outside through symmetrical, vaulted stairways at the two extremities. Smaller flights of stairs lead from it to the *summa cavaea*. In other openings there were seats and windows facing the outside. The wall of one of them bears the following love inscription, painted in large red letters: *non amo te / mereris* or "I don't love you. Do you deserve it?" (meaning my love). Above is an 18th-century signature in red paint. The aforementioned light shaft can also be admired, this time from above, paying some attention to the 18th-century *piperno* balcony.

The *cavaea* seats were made of local tuff blocks, but upgrading works were in progress in the Theatre at the time of the eruption. By one of the seven narrow radial stepped ramps the visitors can descend to the orchestra, which is marble-paved as are the side-boxes (*tribunalia*) for important persons, barred by marble transennae. Facing the visitors is the stage-front, built of marble-clad bricks, mostly restored in the 18th century, in the shape of an alternate series of semicircular and rectangular recesses, each being separated from its neighbour by a short straight-fronted section. Laterally, on the three low steps preceding the VIP boxes, the curule seats and movable bronze chairs were placed for other distinguished spectators. The posthumous dedications to the Augustan age senator, praetor and governor of Crete and Cyrene, *M. Nonius Balbus,* and the one to Cicero's friend and consul (in 38 B.C.) *Appius Claudius Pulcher* can be seen here. Climbing one of the small stairways to the scene one realizes that this is mostly occupied by two large pylons erected by La Vega in the 18th century to support the ceiling of the huge cavern, still extant, created by the excavations.

One of the stairways of Herculaneum Theatre

94

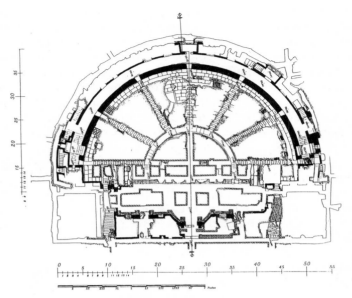

Herculaneum Theatre plan

Alcubierre feared in fact that in the event of an earthquake the overlying houses might collapse, and thus he ordered that the ceiling of the cave be prodded up. The brickwork wall of the stage-building (*scenae frons*), panelled with marble (only fragments of the latter remain) and adorned with rectangular niches and a projecting socle, can be observed here. It contains the three traditional doorways of the Roman theatre, the *porta regia* in the central apse, and the two lateral smaller *portae hospitales*. Cross-sections of the carbonized beams of the collapsed roof, some still in position, can be noticed looking upwards. Two marble capitals, just roughly hewn at the back, are exposed here. Behind and to the left of the *porta regia* there is a tunnel: at a certain point of the ceiling there is, imprinted in the tuff, the head of a statue of M. Nonius Balbus, which was found in 1768, toppled from its pedestal, now in the National Archaeological Museum in Naples (inv. no. 6102). The tunnel leads to the hole dug in 1710, the starting point of the Bourbon era excavations, begun in 1738. Also behind the stage was a portico siding à lower-lying clearing, where Weber wrongly claimed that the marble equestrian statues of the *Nonii Balbi*, now in the atrium of the above said Museum, along with fragments of another equestrian bronze statue of M. Nonius Balbus with its inscription, and two colossal marble statues, were found. Newly discovered contempory documents demonstrate instead that these statues were unearthed in the so-called Basilica.

95

Entering the *versurae* (projecting wings of the stage building) several fragments of elegant pictorial decorations, done on a red and white background in the IV style, and repairs to damage inflicted by the 62 A.D. earthquake — such as a completely re-built arch — can be seen. Another feature is represented by the signatures of hundreds of visitors from various parts of the world, dating from the18th century onwards, which "adorn" the walls. The most recent are from the 2nd World War times, when the underground monument was used, during Allied air raids, as a bomb shelter. From this point one can take a walk around the outside of the Theatre, with its massive brick piers: in two places, sounded out on request of the "Accademia Ercolanese", the entire heigth of the monument, with its two arcade orders, is on view. The next-to-last arcade, finely decorated with pilaster strips, stucco capitals and stucco caissons in the intrados, has in its far side a marble-panelled podium: here d'Alcubierre discovered three togaed male statues. A niche in the courtyard of the former Royal Palace in Portici still houses one of them.

Emerging from the subterranean visit and taking the facing road (Via Fontana) it is possible to look at the picturesque open-air market of Pugliano, which developed immediately after the end of WW2 to deal with discarded American clothes (established when times were hard, it is now mostly visited by expatriate guest-workers and by hunters of fashionable "antiques" at bargain prices); the place is dominated by the elegant belfry and church of S.Maria di Pugliano, mediaeval in origin but re-built in the16th century. Five centuries earlier this territory, named *Plagiense*, was still part (until 1154) of the Byzantine Neapolitan Duchy, this being the reason why two re-used Roman sarcophagi hosted inside bear 11th-century Greek inscriptions.

From the Theatre exit, turning left instead, the Bourbon Royal Palace of Portici, currently the seat of the Faculty of Agrarian Sciences of the Naples University, can be reached. In the last few years restoration of the top ("noble") floor has started, rich in remarkably beautiful pavements (two of them being ancient mosaics), frescoes and stucco decorations, bearing witness to the former splendour of this residence, erected by Charles of Bourbon and his wife Mary Amalia of Saxony, both enchanted by the beauty of the place.

The M. Nonius Balbus inscription on one of the Theater's boxes

THE NEW EXCAVATIONS
OF THE VILLA OF THE PAPYRI

On the west side of the city of Herculaneum, beyond the river mentioned by the Roman historian Sisenna, rises a monumental seaside residence, the Villa of the Papyri, once extending for over 250 metres on the edge of a shore-facing cliff. The villa gets its name from the discovery of more than 1,000 scrolls, mostly in Greek (only a few are in Latin) and some waxed tablets on which probably some musical notations were written. Casually discovered in 1750, it was explored through burrows until 1764 by Karl Weber, who drew up an accurate plan of it, enriched with, by now, precious remarks. Besides the papyri, splendid mosaic floors, remarkable fresco remains and, above all, complete marble and bronze sculptural cycles were found in the villa. These are currently displayed in some of the halls of the National Archaeological Museum in Naples.

The dimensions of the villa are very impressive: the large peristyle, with 25 columns on each of the longer sides and 10 on the shorter sides, was just a bit less than 100m long and 37m wide, with a pool in the centre more than 66m in length.

As to the name of its erudite owner, various hypotheses have been advanced. The one that has gained more credit, based on the presence of works by the Epicurean philosopher Philodemos, who was a client of the owner, is that the owner was the very rich *L. Calpurnius Piso Cesoninus,* Iulius Caesar's father-in-law and Roman consul in 58 B.C. To this possibility the German historian Theodore Mommsen opposed the evidence that no freedmen with this person's name appeared to be living in Herculaneum. Recently, however, a bronze portrait, found in the city and most probably in the villa itself, has been identified as that of Cesonino's son, *L. Calpurnius Piso Pontifex,* consul in 15 B.C., who died in 32. The latter has also been suggested as a possible owner of the patrician villa. Another hypothesis, in our opinion more convincing, is to consider *Appius Claudius Pulcher* the owner of the villa. Consul in 15 B.C. and Cicero's friend, he was imbued with Greek culture, and certainly had interests in Herculaneum territory, as attested by two theatre inscriptions. It is also no longer a sustainable argument to oppose such identification, as has been attempted, because of the lack of *Claudii* freedmen, since many were the local *Claudii,* even of a high social standing.

The villa has been totally reproduced, in the United States, in the J. P. Getty Museum in Malibu (California). It consists of the following parts: 1) The Atrium Quarter; 2) The Smaller Peristyle; 3) The Eastern Living Quarter with the Papyri Library and the Bathroom; 4) The Large Peristyle on the western side; 5) The Garden with some rooms and, at its extremity, the Belvedere rotunda.

Recently a programme has been started which aims to bringing the villa to full light. A deep, narrow trench was dug, starting from Aristide's House, following the ancient sea-front with a gallery underpassing Via Mare. Part of a large building, with halls and a thermal room, was excavated: it shows a terrace decorated on the top with a line of rectangular niches. More excavations were carried out in the southwestern extremity of the city, with the discovery of houses being renovated at the time of the eruption (in one of the rooms the wall decorations were in the process of being remade). Also discovered was a colonnaded courtyard, a rectangular fountain and a thermal complex with a big rectangular apse-ended nimphaeum. In a large room with architectural IV-style formal decorations, a Neo-attic marble bas-relief was found, set in the eastern wall and depicting a nymph drawing water from a lion-headed fountain, a Satyr sitting on a rock and drinking, and another Satyr pouring water into a crater. The buildings are arranged on two staggered terraces.

Finally the atrium area of Villa of the Papyri was unearthed. It shows a well preserved mosaic flooring with fine polychrome geometric decorations and remains of beautiful II-style drawings. A seaward colonnaded terrace is plastered white, and below is another terrace where, surmounted by round windows (*oculi*), are the entrances to other rooms belonging to the lower floor. In two of the atrium rooms, on the collapsing upper-level storeys, a great quantity of wheat grains were found.

From the remainder of the villa some 18th-century tunnels have been cleared of earth, up to the library and the belvedere.

The area of works in progress is still closed to the public. In spite of the large amount of money invested in the project, the aim of bringing the lordly, grandiose villa completely to light is still unachieved, as it is still necessary to expropriate large overhead plots of land and above all to resort to a renewed and more pondered commitment. The complete excavation of the villa remains one of the priority enterprises in Vesuvian archaeology.

In the most recent period, during the exploration of a room in mixed reticulate- and brick-work located on the southeast side of the atrium (but it is yet to be ascertained whether the room actually belongs to the villa) a beautiful marble statue was discovered, apparently an elaborate copy of the Augustan age "Hera Borghese" model. Also discovered was a head, being a copy of the Amazon commonly ascribed to the classic sculptor Kresilas.

THE HERCULANEUM PAPYRI

The charred papyri rolls were found, in the period between October 1752 and August 1754, in five different parts of the building, but mainly in one of the rooms where there were also some cabinets decorated with little bronze busts of philosophers. Initially the rolls were thought to be wood stumps, but they were soon recognised as papyri, whereupon the Bourbon diggers carefully recovered the delicate find, numbering more than 1,000 rolls. There were various failed attempts to open them, such as that by C. Paderni, who employed a knife, or through alchemic methods such as those attempted by the famous Prince of Sansevero, Raimondo di Sangro, and others. As expected, they only caused damage to some of the better preserved rolls. Thanks to the good offices of Giuseppe Assemani, Prefect of the Vatican Library, a Scolopian Father by the name of Antonio Piaggio was at least sent to Naples. He was an expert calligrapher from Genoa, who invented a device to safely unroll the papyri. The system was very slow: after smearing the roll with a gluey substance, Piaggio tied strips of ox bladder on it. These strips were connected to silk strings which were pulled by a system of hooks. The traction produced the gradual unrolling of the papyri.

All the Herculaneum papyri are at present preserved in the Papyri Workshop of the Naples National Library located in the former Royal Palace, with the exception of two specimens which have been transferred to the hall dedicated to the Villa of the Papyri in the National Archaeological Museum in Naples. A few more, donated to Napoleon in 1802, are now in the Louvre, while some more, which are now in London, were given to the Prince of Wales (later King George IV) in 1816, in recognition of his full commitment the task of having the Herculaneum library opened, interpreted and published.

Among the readable papyri only 57 are in Latin, the others in Greek. The most important of the first group contain a poetic work on the Aziac war, probably by the Augustan-age poet *L. Varius Rufus*. Moreover, there are two fragments of what could be prayers, and recently some excerpts from the works of Lucretius and Ennius have been found.

The Greek works are all philosophical in content and for the most part related to the Epicurean school of thought. The rolls can be dated from the 3rd-2nd century B.C. to the first years of our era. Here is a list of some of the most important.

By Epicurus (341-270 B.C.), three copies of the fundamental work, divided in 37 books, *"About Nature"*, completely unknown before the Herculaneum discovery, plus some other works.

By Epicurus' favourite disciple, Metrodorus, only the title of one of his works was preserved in the collection: *"About Wealth"*.

By Kolotes, another pupil, two polemical works: *"Against Plato's Lysis"* and *"Against Plato's Eutidemos"*.

By Karneiskos, also one of Epicurus' pupils, we have *"Philistes"*, a work exalting the epicurean idea of friendship.

By Polistratos, who led the Athenian epicurean school in the second part of the 3rd century B.C., we have two works, one is *"About Philosophy"*, made up of at least two books, the other is *"About Irrational Contempt of Public Opinions"*, written against antagonist philosophers.

By Demetrius Lako, an Epicurean who lived in the 2nd century B.C., the following works *"About Poetry"*, *"About Geometry"*, *"About Polyenos' Apories"*, *"About Epicurus Sentences"*, *"About Subjects Considered for Common Research in a Philosophical Meeting"*. Other papyri deal with various philosophical subjects and are of uncertain paternity.

Philodemos, an Epicurean philosopher who lived between the end of the 2nd and the second half of the 1st century B.C., is present in such an important way that it is possible to argue this was the library he used himself.

In the collection the philosopher Krisippos, who led the Stoic School in the second part of the 2nd century B.C., is also represented with the first two books of his *"About Providence"*, a book regarding *"Logical Researches"* and a work on ethics.

Another papyrus in Latin (inventory no. 1806) was found in Herculaneum in 1870, but unfortunately it is not known where. Since 1969 the "International Centre for the Study of the Herculaneum Papyri" founded and directed by prof. Marcello Gigante, who excels in Herculanean studies, has been operating in Naples. Gigante is committed to the research and publication of the scrolls and is also to be credited with promoting the resumption of excavations in the huge Villa of the Papyri. He is the editor of the yearly journal *"Cronache Ercolanesi"* specifically dedicated to papyrology and to Herculaneum archaeology, as well as the book series *"La Scuola di Epicuro"*.

The recent excavations in Villa of the Papyri, although focused on the library area, have not brought to light, up to press time, any other rolls. This notwithstanding, Herculaneum and its territory for sure still keep hidden many other treasures of ancient culture.

Nero's golden coin (versus and back)

THE SEVENTEENTH CENTURY
VILLA CAMPOLIETO

Once out of the excavations, if the visitor turns right, he will walk along a tract of the road which goes from Naples to Calabria known as *Il Miglio d'oro* (The Golden Mile), because of the splendour of the landscape and the great number of beautiful villas belonging to Neapolitan high society. This was a preferred residential estate also due to the closeness to the Capital and to the Royal Palace in Portici, one of the Bourbon kings' summer residences. After a very short distance, to the right, there is the seventeenth century Villa de Bisogno belonging to the Marquis of Casaluce, with a nice decorated façade. Proceeding forward, on the left is the long front-side of Villa Aprile, previously Riario Sforza, belonging to the famous Austrian General Laval Nugent (who had married a lady of the Riario Sforza family). He was a passionate antiques' collector, and at his own expense he carried out the archaeological excavations in Minturno: his collections are now kept in the Zagreb Museum. The villa is privately owned and has a beautiful park with imitation ruins and a round fountain with a statue of Neptune, visible from the open entrance hall.

Continuing further, after the intersection with *Via dei Quattro Orologi* on the right there is one of the most splendid 17th century villas, which has been completely restored in recent times thanks to efforts of the the "Vesuvian Villas Foundation"; a visit is usually possible every morning, except on holidays.

Villa Campolieto was built in 1755 by the Duke of Casacalenda, who initially entrusted the project and the execution of the work to architect Mario Gioffredo, who opted for a square-base building with a central gallery in the form of a Greek cross. On the back he planned a circular portico-belvedere, opening on the seaward side, and made arrangements for the stables and the coach-house. Around 1760 Gioffredo quit the direction of the works because of a disagreement with the owner, and he was replaced, between 1763 and 1773, by Luigi Vanvitelli. After the death of this most celebrated architect the work was brought to completion, in 1775, under the direction of his son Carlo.

Luigi Vanvitelli vastly renewed the original project: he transformed the monumental staircase, enlarging its previous size, and modified the design of the belvedere-terrace interrupting its perimeter at the extremities of the back façade, along which he built a straight portico. He also changed the plan of the colonnaded area from round to elliptical.

In front and below the elliptical belvedere there is a fish-pond fountain and the vista dramatically widens seaward on to the Gulf of Naples. On the eastern side of the belvedere the stables, containing a collection of antique coaches, are located.

The most important painting decorations which can be admired in the living quarters of the building (upper floor) are the following:

In the vestibule: 4 medallions depicting the four seasons and mythological scenes, by Crescenzo La Gamba.

In the gallery on the right: Minerva and Mercury framed in a splendid and airy colonnade, by Jacopo Cestaro.

In the halls to the right of the gallery: in two communicating rooms, Aurora and little winged cupids, huntress Diana and Apollo with a lyre by Jacopo Cestaro, beside various ornamental motifs, some echoing Pompeiian models.

In the central dining hall, very elegant decorations by Fedele Fischetti and Gaetano Magri, with garden scenes and people.

In the gallery on the left (party hall): architectural elements, festoons, statues, medallions with mythological scenes, also by Fischetti and Magri.

A large terrace spreads out towards the sea.

The period of glory of Villa Campolieto was very short due to the debts contracted by the owners and the extinction of the main family branch with the passing away of Scipione di Sangro in 1805.

Villa Campolieto as seen from the seaside

THE ROMAN WALL-PAINTING TECHNIQUE

The Roman wall paintings surprise both the scholars and the modern interested public, not only for their high artistic quality and imagination inherent to the decorations and pictured subjects (in spite of the fact that it was a widespread craft, as attested by the abundant documentation provided by the Vesuvian area) but also for its extraordinary technical perfection. Compared to the Mediaeval and Renaissance frescoes, the Roman technique shows superior smoothness and resistance of the painted surfaces, along with a greater brilliance and durability of the colours.

The method used to reach such results has been the object of research and debate since the 18th century, and is still partly open, even though it is widely accepted that we are dealing basically with frescoes.

The ancient writers, mainly Vitruvius and Pliny, discussed the way painted wall plasters were made, and how the colours were produced and mixed. Besides the splendid examples of the Vesuvian area, we have an ever-increasing number of wall decorations from Rome, from the rest of Italy and from the Empire's provinces. It is interesting to note the direct evidence of how the painters' work progressed, due to the fact that it was left at various stages of completion in the Vesuvian area because of the eruption — as in the Iliac Sacellum House and in the Caste Lovers House in Pompeii, and in the Pretty Courtyard House and in the new excavation of Villa of the Papyri in Herculaneum.

Painstaking surveys and research on Roman paintings in the Vesuvian district have also led to the recognition of a series of schools which grouped together decorative methods and themes — to form an idea about the sequential development of tastes and preferences, all within the framework provided by the fundamental division in four styles established by the great German scholar August Mau.

Roman wall painting was essentially done in fresco. The main trait of the procedure was to apply the colours on lime plaster before it hardened. When hardening of the mortar was complete, the colour appeared well soaked through, and bonded to, the surface layer of calcium carbonate produced by the reaction of lime with the carbon dioxide in the air. Vitruvius describes this process exactly: "if the colours are carefully laid on the wet plaster they will never fade out, they will be permanently preserved". It is necessary, then, for the painter to have a layer of preparation plaster still wet, and to work as quickly as possible on a limited area, competently handling the junction strips resulting from such work phases.

Vitruvius describes the execution of a wall painting in detail, preceded by seven successive preparation layers: one of rough wall smoothing, three lime and sand floating coats, and three other coats with very fine-grained lime and marble powder upon which, after an appropriate smoothing process, the colour itself was applied. Since we can only distinguish four layers at most (Vitruvius himself mentions thinner plasters and fewer layers — as we can see in the actual paintings — particularly in the less important areas), it is generally believed that the description of this Augustan-age architect was purely theoretical, derived from the Hellenistic technical literature which he used a lot.

The good quality of materials, the accuracy and thickness of the preparation layers, the smoothing with trowels, rolls and other tools, consented a remarkable technical perfection, but also a slow drying of plaster which improved the quality of the intervening coats of paint. The colours added to those already applied in the background were mixed with lime if applied when the support plaster was still wet, which was done in order to renew the calcium carbonate reaction. The general result, in fact, was a strong chemical bond with the wall plaster, almost as strong as the background colour underneath. Some colours did not tolerate lime causticity, so they are not to be found in wall paintings. Vitruvius and Pliny mention a glue paste used to apply black colouring, and a preserving treatment with "Punic wax" (wax melted in saltwater), diluted with oil, heated on coals contained in an iron vase and finally rubbed with clean rags on cinnabar (the famous Pompeiian red). Cinnabar was among the most expensive and appreciated colours, but subject to rapid alteration in case of humidity combined with light. Pliny also states that painters used to mix *Murex*-red with eggs. It cannot be ruled out that in other cases too, some kind of gluten was used to ensure colour durability, but its exact nature is hard to tell.

The painters started working from the top down: the ceiling was painted first, followed by the stucco wall-frames, then, in succession, the upper side of the walls (frieze), the central area, and finally the baseboard. Often the separation line between the various workdays stands right at the junction of these different areas. In larger rooms vertical sutures were necessary, but they were always accurately concealed. Flooring the room was always the last step.

Depending on their specialisation the painters had different names: the *dealbator* whitewashed the walls and laid the background colour of the decoration. The *parietarius* outlined and executed repetitive panels and decorations, though with some sort of variation. Generally the *imaginarii* were last, the better-paid artists who painted the central part of the walls with picture-drawings. The areas reserved to them were left undone and very slightly recessed so they could initially make preliminary sketches with watercolours and then paint the drawings on freshly laid plaster. The central picture drawings were often derived from famous Greek models. Because of their value, they were at times recovered from previous decorations or even painted elsewhere and then set in place in wooden frames, as seen in two Herculaneum places, a house on the *decumanus maximus* and the Palaestra. Several painters often worked simultaneously on more than one wall, driven by the need to execute the decoration before the preparation layers were completely dry. It is often possible to notice instances of thread-beating on the fresh plaster in order to outline architectural partitions, preliminary contours with diluted colours, tracings and appliqué drawings for the pictures to be done.

Appendix No. 2

THE "POMPEIIAN STYLES" OF PAINTING

The so-called Pompeiian styles, defined in the 19th century by the great German archaeologist August Mau and subjected to several intervening studies and refinements, express fashion and taste patterns which evolved in the parietal decoration of Pompeii from the Hellenistic age up to the destruction of the city.

I style - Introduced from Greece, where it is documented since the 4th century B.C., it is carachterized by vividly-painted stucco imitations of the rich marble revetments of the royal and aristocratic residences. In due time, even some decorative details such as listels and ovoids, friezes with garlands, meanders, and less often, beehive-motives with softly-coloured figures, were represented.
II style - Introduced in Pompeii at the time of the Sillan colony, the II style imaginatively transforms the architectural partitions of the I style, attributing an illusion of depth to the surface of the walls with the perspective of colonnades and ceilings, and with views of sanctuaries, landscapes and cityscapes drawn behind fully-open doors and porticoes. In many instances it is clear that the style is inspired by the rich theatre scenes then in vogue. In a later development, the compositions sort of sober up, with the adoption of simpler pictorial schemes.
III style - It is connected to the Augustan-age classicism and implies the "closure" of the surfaces of the walls, contrary to their elaborate, fanciful treatment of the II style. On the ample, brilliant light-monochrome surfaces, bordered with thin lines, amid graceful candelabra, tripods

and colonnettes, lovely flying figurines stand out. The central shrines are often occupied by animated paintings derived from famous prototypes. Occasionally, Egyptian figurative elements also show up.

IV style - It originates during Nero's age in the magnificent decorations of the imperial and aristocratic palaces, and it is documented at its best in Pompeii owing to the wast refurbishing works that followed the 62 A.D. earthquake. In a first phase, representations imitating hanging carpets, bordered by finely-executed vignettes, prevail. There follows a reprise of the II-style illusionism, when "baroque" architectural scenes, crowded by emblematic figures, heroes, gods, athletes, and statues, set in. The taste for animated paintings in the central shrines still persists. Yet some decorations exhibit a stiffness typical of the III style, with vertical and horizontal elements outweighing the others, and with stereotype motives ornamenting vast coloured areas.

Herculaneum papyrus (*Philodemus about music*)

BIBLIOGRAPHY

Inventories

G.P. ZOTTOLI, *Bibliografia Ercolanese*, edited by A. MAIURI, in *Bollettino Istituto Nazionale di Archeologia e Storia dell'arte*, II, 1938, pp. 3-37.

I.C. McILWAINE, *Herculaneum. A Guide to Printed Sources*, Naples 1988, with a supplement in *Cronache Ercolanesi*, 20, 1990, pp. 87-128.

L. GARCIA Y GARCIA, *Nova bibliotheca Pompeiana. 250 anni di bibliografia archeologica*, Roma 1998.

The Eruption

H. SIGURDSSON – S. CASHDOLLAR – S.R.J. SPARKS, *The Eruption of Vesuvius in a.d. 79: Reconstruction from Historical and Volcanological Evidence*, in *American Journal of Archeology*, 86, 1982, pp. 39-57.

H. SIGURDSSON – S. CAREY – W. CORNELL – T. PESCATORE, *The Eruption of Vesuvius in a.D. 79*, in *National Geographic Research*, I, 3, 1985, pp. 332-387.

R. SANTACROCE (ed.), *Somma-Vesuvius*, Roma 1987.

U. PAPPALARDO, *L'eruzione pliniana del Vesuvio nel 79 d. C.: Ercolano*, in *Volcanologie et Archéologie*, PACT. 25, Strasbourg 1990, pp. 197-215.

E. RENNA, *Vesuvius mons*, Napoli 1992.

A. NAZZARO, *Il Vesuvio*, Napoli 1997.

G. LUONGO (ed.), *Mons Vesuvius*, Napoli 1997.

History of the Excavations

S. D'ALOE, *Degli scavamenti ercolanesi nel secol presente*, in *Annali civili del Regno delle Due Sicilie*, 49, fasc. 94, 1853, pp. 107-115 e fasc. 97, pp. 14-18.

M. RUGGIERO, *Storia degli Scavi di Ercolano*, Napoli 1885.

CH. WALDSTEIN – L. SHOOBRIDGE, *Ercolano, passato, presente e futuro*, Torino 1910.

V. CATALANO, *Antiquarium Herculanense*, Napoli 1957.

E. CORTI, *Ercolano e Pompei*, it. transl., Torino 1957.

ARCHIVISTI NAPOLETANI, *Fonti documentarie per la storia degli scavi di Pompei*, Ercolano e Stabia, Napoli 1979.

F. ZEVI, *Gli Scavi di Ercolano*, in *Civiltà del '700 a Napoli*, II, Napoli 1980, pp. 58-68.

J.J. WINCKELMANN, *Le scoperte di Ercolano*, F. STRAZZULLO (ed.), Napoli 1983.

CH. GRELL, *Herculanum et Pompeii dans les recits des voyageurs français du XVIIIe siècle*, Naples 1983, pp. 159-410.

U. PANNUTI, *Il giornale degli scavi di Ercolano (1738-1756)*, in *Mem. Acc. Linc*, sc. morali, ser. VIII, vol XXVI, fasc. 3, Roma 1983, pp. 159-410.

CH. PARSLOW, *Rediscovering Antiquity. Karl Weber and the Excavation of Herculaneum, Pompeii and Stabiae*, Cambridge Mass. 1995.

G. MAGGI, *Ercolano. Fine di una città*, Napoli 1985.

M. PAGANO, *La scoperta di Ercolano*, in *Il Vesuvio e le città vesuviane 1730-1860*, Atti del Convegno di Studi, 1996, pubbl. Napoli 1998, pp. 47-74 (cfr. *Rivista di Studi Pompeiani*, IX, 1998, pp. 107-119).

M. PAGANO, *I diari di scavo di Pompei, Ercolano e Stabiae di Francesco e Pietro La Vega (1764-1810)*, Roma 1997.

M.FORCELLINO, *Camillo Paderni Romano e l'immagine storica degli scavi di Pompei, Ercolano e Stabia*, Roma 1999.

Guidebooks

A. MAIURI, *Ercolano*, 4th edition, Roma 1954.
M. BRION, *Pompéi et Herculanum*, Paris 1965.
G. CERULLI IRELLI, *Ercolano*, Cava dei Tirreni 1969.
A. DE FRANCISCIS, *Ercolano e Stabia*, Novara 1974.
A. and M. DE VOS, *Pompei, Ercolano, Stabia*, Guide archeologiche Laterza, Bari 1982.
J. J. DEISS, *Herculaneum*, Malibu 1989.
T. BUDETTA, *Ercolano*, Ercolano 1991, ed. 1998.
J. J. DEISS, *The town of Hercules*, Malibu 1995.

Topography, Town-planning, Architecture, Building Techniques

A. MAIURI, *Oecus Aegyptius*, in *Studies presented to D. Moore Robinson*, I, Washington 1951, pp. 423-429.
A. MAIURI, *Oeci vitruviani in Palladio e nella Casa pompeiana ed ercolanese*, in *Palladio*, 1-2, 1952, pp. 1-8.
A. MAIURI, *Ercolano. I Nuovi Scavi*, I, Roma 1958.
V. CATALANO, *Case, abitanti e culti di Ercolano*, Napoli 1966.
G. CERULLI IRELLI, *La casa del 'colonnato tuscanico' ad Ercolano*, Napoli 1974.
F. MIELKE, *Scale ad Ercolano*, in *Antiqua*, I, 3, 1976, pp. 45-53.
E. SALZA PRINA RICOTTI, *Cucine in epoca romana*, in *Rendiconti della pontificia accademia romana di archeologia*, 51-52, 1978-80, pp. 237-294.
G. GUADAGNO, *Herculanensium Augustalium aedes* in *Cronache Ercolanesi*, 13, 1983, pp. 159-173.
TRAN TAN TIHN, *La Casa dei Cervi à Herculanum*, Roma 1988.
TH. GANSCHOW, *Untersuchungen zur Baugeschichte in Herculaneum*, Bonn 1989.
E. DE ALBENTIIS, *La casa dei Romani*, Milano 1990.
M. PAGANO, *Ercolano. Saggi all'interno dell'area urbana*, in *Bollettino di Archeologia*, I, 3, 1990, pp. 125-128.
R. DE KIND, *The Study of Houses at Herculaneum*, in *BABesch*, 66, 1991, pp. 175-185.
J. R. CLARKE, *The Houses of Roman Italy*, Oxford 1991.
J. DE WAELE – R. DE KIND – C. PETERSE, *Case di Pompei ed Ercolano: disegno e progettazione*, in *Opuscula Pompeiana*, VI, Kyoto 1996, pp. 1-16.
A. WALLACE – HADRILL, *Houses and society* in *Pompeii and Herculaneum*, Princeton 1994.
M. PAGANO, *La nuova pianta della città e di alcuni edifici pubblici di Ercolano*, in *Cronache Ercolanesi*, 26, 1996, pp. 229-262.
M. PAGANO – T. PESCATORE-F. RIPPA, *The coast in the area of the Herculaneum excavations at the time of the Romans*, in *Geotechnical engineering for the preservation of monuments and historic sites*, C. VIGGIANI (ed.), Balkema, Rotterdam 1997, pp. 759-766.
R. DE KIND, *Houses in Herculaneum*, Amsterdam 1998.
U. PAPPALARDO, *Die Suburbanen Thermen von Herculaneum*, in *Antike Welt*, 30, 3, 1999, pp. 209-218.

Frescoes and floors

G. CERULLI IRELLI, *Le pitture della casa dell'Atrio a Mosaico, Monumenti della pittura antica scoperti in Italia*, s. 3, fasc. I, Roma 1971.
M. MANNI, *Le pitture della casa del colonnato tuscanico, Monumenti della pittura antica scoperti in Italia*, s. 3, fasc. II, Roma 1974.
M. MANNI, *Per la storia della pittura ercolanese*, in *Cronache Ercolanesi*, 20, 1990, pp. 129-143.
F. GUIDOBALDI – F. OLEVANO – D. TRUCCHI, *Sectilia pavimenta di Ercolano: classificazione e confronto con il campione pompeiano*, in *VI Coloquio Internacional sobre el mosaico antiquo*, Valencia-Mérida 1990, Guadalajara 1994, pp. 63-71.

F. GUIDOBALDI – F. OLEVANO, *Sectilia pavimenta dall'area vesuviana*, in *Marmi antichi II. Cave e tecnica di lavorazione, provenienze e distribuzione*, P. PENSABENE (ed.), *Studi Miscellanei*, 31, Roma 1998, pp. 223-240.

Wooden Furniture

T. BUDETTA – M. PAGANO, *Legni e bronzi di Ercolano. Testimonianze dell'arredo e delle suppellettili della casa romana*, Catalogo della mostra, Roma 1988.

S.T.A.M. MOLS, *Wooden furniture in Herculaneum. Form, Technique and Function*, Amsterdam 1999.

Inscriptions

M. DELLA CORTE – P. SOPRANO, *Onomasticon Herculanense*, in R*endiconti dell'Accademia di Archeologia*, Lettere e Belle Arti, n. s. 27, 1952, pp. 211-233.

M. DELLA CORTE, *Le iscrizioni di Ercolano*, in *Rendiconti dell'Accademia di Archeologia, Lettere e Belle Arti*, n. s. 33, 1958, pp. 239-308.

G. GUADAGNO, *Supplemento epigrafico ercolanese I*, in *Cronache Ercolanesi* 8, 1978, pp. 132-155 e II, in *Cronache Ercolanesi*, 11, 1981, pp. 129-164.

Archives of Waxed Tablets and Various Objects

A. MAIURI, *Tabulae ceratae herculanenses*, in *La Parola del Passato*, I, 1946, pp. 373-379.

G. CAMODECA, *Per una riedizione delle tabulae herculanenses*, I, in *Cronache Ercolanesi*, 23, 1993, pp. 109-119.

A. DE FRANCISCIS, *Vetri antichi scoperti ad Ercolano*, in *Journal of Glass Studies*, 5, 1963, pp. 137-139.

G. CAMODECA, *Per una riedizione delle tabulae herculanenses*, II, in *Ostraka*, 2, 1993, pp. 197-209.

G. CAMODECA, *La ricostruzione dell'élite municipale ercolanese degli anni 50-70: problemi di metodo e risultati preliminari*, in *Cahiers Glotz*, VII, 1996, pp. 167-178.

A.M. BISI INGRASSIA, *Le lucerne fittili dei nuovi scavi di Ercolano*, in *L'instrumentum domesticum di Ercolano e Pompei nella prima età imperiale*, Roma 1977, pp. 73-104.

L.A. SCATOZZA HORICHT, *I vetri romani di Ercolano*, Roma 1986.

M. CONTICELLO DE SPAGNOLIS – E. DE CAROLIS, *Le lucerne di bronzo di Ercolano e Pompei*, Roma 1988.

L.A. SCATOZZA HORICHT, *I monili di Ercolano*, Roma 1989.

L.J. BUQUEZ, *Roman Surgical Instruments and other Minor Objects in the National Archaeological Museum of Naples*, Mainz 1994.

E. DE CAROLIS, *Ceramica comune da mensa e da dispensa di Ercolano*, in *Les ceramiques communes de Campanie et de Narbonnaise (Ier s. av. J.C. – Ier s. ap. J.C.)*, Napoli 1996, pp. 121-128.

L.A. SCATOZZA HORICHT, *Appunti sulla ceramica comune di Ercolano. Vasellame da cucina e recipienti per la preparazione degli alimenti, ibidem*, pp. 129-156.

M. PAGANO, *Tegulae Campanae ad Ercolano*, in *Cronache Ercolanesi*, 20, 1990, pp. 157-176.

A. D'AMBROSIO – E. DE CAROLIS (ed.), *I monili dall'area vesuviana*, Roma 1997.

Foodstuff

F. G. MEYER, *Food plants identified from carbonized remains*, in *Studia Pompeiana and classica in honor of W. F. Jashemski*, I, New York 1988, pp. 183-200, anche in *Economic Botany*, 34, 1980.

A. DOSI – F. SCHNELL, *A tavola con i Romani antichi*, Roma 1984.

M. PAGANO, *Commercio e consumo del grano ad Ercolano*, in *Le ravaitaillement en blé de Rome et des centres urbains des débuts de la République jusqu'au Haut Empire*, Naples-Romes 1994, pp. 141-147.

E. SALZA PRINA RICOTTI, *Ricette della cucina romana a Pompei e come eseguirle*, Roma 1997.

Villa of the Papyri

D. COMPARETTI – G. DE PETRA, *La villa ercolanese dei Pisoni. I suoi monumenti e la sua biblioteca*, Torino 1883.

M. GIGANTE, *Catalogo dei papiri ercolanesi*, Napoli 1979.

M. GIGANTE, *Ricerche filodemee*, Napoli 1983.

Contributi alla storia della officina dei papiri ercolanesi 1, Napoli 1980 e 2, Roma 1986.

Indici dei papiri ercolanesi, Terzo Suppl. a Cronache Ercolanesi, Napoli 1993.

AA. VV., *La Villa dei Papiri*, M. GIGANTE (ed.), *Secondo Suppl. Cronache Ercolanesi*, 13, Napoli 1983.

M. GIGANTE, *Contributi alla storia della officina dei papiri ercolanesi*, 1, Napoli 1980 and 2, Roma 1986.

M. GIGANTE, *Philodemos in Italia*, Firenze 1990 (English edition: Ann Arbour 1996).

M.R. WOJCIK, *La Villa dei Papiri ad Ercolano*, Roma 1986.

B. CONTICELLO – A. DE SIMONE, in *Cronache Ercolanesi*, 17, 1987, pp. 9-36.

M. CAPASSO, *Manuale di papirologia ercolanese*, Galatina 1991.

M. GIGANTE, *Epicuro e l'epicureismo nei papiri ercolanesi*, Napoli 1993.

C. BASILE, *I papiri carbonizzati di Ercolano*, Napoli 1994.

A. DE SIMONE et al., Ercolano 1992-1997. *La Villa dei Papiri e lo scavo della città*, in *Cronache Ercolanesi*, 28, 1998, pp. 3-63.

Oriental Cults

TRAN TAM TINH, *Le culte des divinités orientales a Herculanum*, Leiden 1971.

Theatre

M. PAGANO, *Il teatro di Ercolano*, in *Cronache Ercolanesi*, 23, 1993, pp. 121-156.

U. PAPPALARDO, *Nuove testimonianze su Marco Nonius Balbus ad Ercolano*, in *Römische Mitteilungen*, 104, 1997, pp. 417-433.

Fugitive Skeletons and Boat

J.R. STEFFY, *The Herculaneum Boat: Preliminary Notes on Hull Construction*, in *American Journal of Archaeology*, 89, 1985, pp. 519-521.

S.C. BISEL, *Human Bones at Herculaneum*, in *Rivista di Studi Pompeiani*, I, 1987, pp. 123-129.

A.M. FERRONI – C. MEUCCI, *Prime osservazioni sulla barca di Ercolano: il recupero e la costruzione navale*, in *Atti del Convegno "Il restauro del legno"*, I, Firenze 1989, pp. 105-112.

S.C. BISEL, *The Secrets of Vesuvius*, Toronto 1990.

E. DE CAROLIS, *Lo Scavo dei Fornici 7 e 8 sulla Marina di Ercolano*, in *Rivista di Studi Pompeiani*, VI, 1993-94, pp. 167-186.

M. TORINO – G. FORNACIARI, *Analisi dei resti umani dei fornici 7 e 8 sulla marina di Ercolano, ibidem*, pp. 187-195.

M. TORINO-G. FORNACIARI, *Indagine paleodemografica su un campione di popolazione dell'antica Ercolano all'epoca dell'eruzione vesuviana del 79 d. C.*, in *Archivio per l'Antropologia e l'Etnologia*, CXXV, 1995, pp. 99-112.

Restorations

M. PAGANO, *Metodologia dei restauri borbonici a Pompei ed Ercolano*, in *Rivista di Studi Pompeiani*, V, 1991-92, pp. 169-191.

M. PAGANO, *Una legge ritrovata: il progetto di legge per il riordinamento del R. Museo di Napoli e degli Scavi di antichità del 1848 e il ruolo di G. Fiorelli*, in *Archivio Storico per le Province Napoletane*, CXII, 1994, pp. 351-414.

M. PAGANO, *Gli architetti direttori degli Scavi di Pompei: regole e iniziative sul restauro archeologico in epoca borbonica*, in *La cultura del restauro. Teorie e fondatori*, S. CASIELLO (ed.), Venezia 1996, pp. 335-349.

Ancient Villas near Herculaneum

L. A. SCATOZZA HORICHT, *Ville nel territorio ercolanese*, in *Cronache Ercolanesi*, 15, 1985, pp. 131-165.

U. PAPPALARDO-A. LAGI DE CARO-H. SIGURDSSON, *Ercolano, Cava Montone: villa rustica romana distrutta dal Vesuvio*, in *Tremblements de terre, éruptions volcaniques et vie des hommes dans la Campanie antique*, Naples 1986, pp. 95-106.

M. PAGANO, *Torre del Greco. Scavo di una villa rustica*, in *Rivista di Studi Pompeiani*, II, 1988, pp. 240-243.

M. PAGANO, *Torre del Greco, località Cupa Falanga*, in *Rivista di Studi Pompeiani*, III, 1989, pp. 285 s.

F. FORMICOLA-U. PAPPALARDO-G. ROLANDI-F. RUSSO, *Archeologia, geologia e vulcanologia nel territorio di Torre del Greco: tre discipline a confronto*, in *Volcanologie et Archéologie*, PACT 25, Strasbourg 1990, pp. 125-181.

M. PAGANO, *La villa romana di contrada Sora a Torre del Greco*, in *Cronache Ercolanesi*, 21, 1991, pp. 149-186.

M. PAGANO, *Pollena Trocchia. Scavo in località masseria De Carolis e ricognizioni nel territorio*, in *Rivista di Studi Pompeiani*, V, 1991-92, pp. 231-236.

M. PAGANO, *Torre del Greco. Notizie varie*, in *Rivista di Studi Pompeiani*, VI, 1993-94, pp. 253-271.

M. PAGANO, *L'area vesuviana dopo l'eruzione del 79 d. C.*, in *Rivista di Studi Pompeiani*, VII, 1995-96, pp. 35-44.

M. PAGANO, *Portici archeologica*, Portici 1997.

Bronze *signacula* (stamps) of *M.Co.Fru.* and *A. Fuferius*

CONTENTS

Printing
SBR srl, via Roma 56a
I-80055 Portici, Naples (Italy)
April 2000